THEOLOGICALLY COMPETENT - PRACTICALLY RELEVANT

IGNITING GRACE

Living and serving in the power of God

by Johannes Justus

Originally published in German under the title: *Entfachende Gnade. Johannes Justus*

© 2019 Copyright Forum Theologie & Gemeinde (FThG) im Bund Freikirchlicher Pfingstgemeinden KdöR, Erzhausen

ISBN (E-book, german)   978-3-942001-34-2

ISBN (pbk, german)   978-3-942001-78-6

Johannes Justus is pastor and former president of the Federation of Pentecostal Free Churches. As an international speaker his knowledge of the Holy Spirit is especially appreciated. His great passion is to promote the development of church congregations in our country. He is particularly interested in the question which role the work of the Holy Spirit plays in the building of church congregations.

For more information visit www.elim-network.de

Johannes Justus

IGNITING GRACE

Cover Design: Daniel Justus

Typesetting: Irena Wick

Translation and Editing: Mirjam Henderson, Erika Rakowski

Published 2023

ISBN (pbk, eng)   978-3-9825978-0-5

Contents

My thanks go to Pastor Albert Stein, Pastor Benjamin Sawadsky, Dr. Rudolf Fichtner and Pastor Daniel Justus for their support in the creation of this work. I would also like to thank my wife, Irene Justus, who has always believed in me, and the many people who have accepted my ministry and allowed me to develop and grow.

FOREWORD

For many years I have been traveling to various places in our country and to other parts of the world to speak to people, to encourage them, and to equip them. It has often happened in the past that after my seminars, lectures and sermons, people have sought me out and asked me where they can read or study what I have said. Unfortunately, it is not always possible to keep what has been said in one's mind and it fades away after a while. So it would be good to have something to read up on. Up to now I could only refer to other literature, which does not contain many of my teaching contents, examples and experiences. Anyway, in recent years I have been increasingly taught that teaching about the Holy Spirit and spiritual gifts is my specialty and that I should write about it. After the BFP Presidium asked me to put my knowledge and my wealth of experience on paper, the idea for this book was born. As I was thinking more about the concept, I realized that it would not be helpful to simply write another book about the Holy Spirit and His work, since there is already a lot of literature on the subject in the Pentecostal movement. However, there is a basic concept in the Bible that has accompanied me all my life and that I believe is central to this topic. It is the grace of God. It was important for me to take a new path with this book and to start from this central concept. Christians often stress the attainability of spiritual life. However, in my perspective, not all aspects of it are within human control, as Holy Scripture indicates that the grace of God is required for spiritual growth and work. This grace of God is vital for spiritual life and activity. It overcomes our heart and leads to our salvation as Christians. It leads us into self-acceptance. It shapes our sense of identity, directing us towards our purpose in life. It is also through grace that we are empowered to serve others. Its function is dynamic, facilitating continual growth. When I deem my audience worthy of trust, I am given the opportunity to discuss the tremendous power of this gift in explicit terms. Thus, I have attempted here to contribute to some much-discussed topics concerning the Holy Spirit. This book is a call to embrace, serve, and grow in God's grace. Starting from the concept of grace, I focus on the gifts of grace. My desire is to open up new thoughts and perspectives for my readers and to liberate God's work through His Spirit from the taint of mystery and enigma that is unjustly attached to it. For years, I have been campaigning in Christianity for us to become spiritual in the natural and natural in the spiritual. This book is meant to serve that purpose. I am aware that many of the thoughts and issues I raise in this book sometimes require deeper explanation. I have not always been able to deal with them in a way that is satisfactory to me. Even the concept of grace[1], which is complex in itself, could not be comprehensively explained in this book. It was more important for me to create a practical work that can be used repeatedly. Therefore, I ask for indulgence from those readers who expected a purely theological analysis. In writing this book, I realized that I needed to move away from some of the boxes and rigid categories in my thinking. The reason for this is the process of change that working on this book has brought about in me. I am grateful for this, and wish and hope that my readers will also experience a little change and grow in grace according to Peter (2 Peter 3:18).

Hanover, spring 2019
Johannes Justus

---

1 *Emil Brunner wrote of grace that it is «the central concept of the Christian biblical knowledge of God». Emil Brunner in: RGG2 II, 1261*

Part 1:
God's grace as a source of trength for life

1   Charis – a small word with great meaning

1.1 Grace in today's culture – familiar and foreign at the same time

Grace is certainly one of the most used terms in the church context. In church services, *God's grace* is thanked and prayed for again and again. It is by grace that we can stand before God, and as fallible human beings we need it anew every day.

As important as the concept of grace is, it has also become overused and abstract. It is now used for all sorts of things, making its true meaning unclear and blurred. For many Christians, *grace has become a pious, empty word*, familiar from church services and used in our own prayers, but it no longer has any special meaning for everyday life. Another contributing factor may be the lack of social relevance of grace, which has little value in contemporary Western culture.

The term grace has become old-fashioned and less present in the secular vocabulary. Apart from its ecclesiastical use, it is almost exclusively found in the legal system or in outdated polite phrases such as *my gracious lady*. This certainly correlates with our current environment. The modern, independent person does not want to receive anything as a gift or to be pardoned. Rather, his desire is to receive what is rightfully his. Influenced by our basic democratic order and political liberalism, we are accustomed to the fact that the sum of individuals governs from the bottom up. The idea of being dependent on the *mercy of an authority* is something negative for the emancipated person. It is therefore not surprising that the concept of grace is becoming more and more alien to today's Western Europeans.

1.2 Grace in the Greek environment in NT times

The term grace (Greek: *charis*) is used in a variety of ways by Paul and the other New Testament writers, as well as in the surrounding Greek Hellenistic context. The short word *charis* thus has a relatively wide range of meanings. Let us first consider the meaning of grace in the pagan environment of the New Testament, so that the differences will become clearer to us. For just as we are subject to the influences of our surrounding culture, the understanding of grace of the NT writers (esp. Paul) was shaped by their environment.

In the Greek environment of the New Testament, the *charis* of the gods described "...a kind of surplus or addition."[2] It was given freely and undeservedly, like a gift. Something that was already good, could be made even better by the *charis*. This form of grace found its expression in the gracefulness, the beauty, and the attractiveness: The gods could make the earthly form appear more attractive. At the same time, the contextual association of *charis* with the term *chara*, meaning "joy", also played a role: Grace stood therefore above all for things that bring joy. The Greeks considered beauty and grace the highest happiness. And nothing fills the heart more than something beautiful that is neither deserved nor expected. This *charis* of the gods, however, was unstable and fragile in its essence. It could only be given to mortals for a limited time. Its beauty sometimes disappeared during life, but at the latest at death. The response of humans to the desired divine grace (*charis*) was also called *charis*. The term thus also included the response that we would describe in today's language as thanksgiving. In summary, the meaning of *charis* in the Greek context of the NT can essentially be described as grace, beauty, gift, favor, and thanksgiving at the same time.

---

2 *Roth: Gnadenlehre, 197.*

1.3 GRACE IN THE GOSPELS

As will become clear in the following text, grace in the NT encompasses more than the above meanings. And even if they did not coin the term themselves, the authors (especially Paul himself) seem to have undertaken a complete redefinition of the term.

In the NT, the term *grace* (*charis*) appears particularly often in the letters of Paul and in the writings of his circle (Luke, Acts), but less so in the Gospels: Jesus himself speaks more of *mercy*. The mercy of God, however, becomes clearly visible and tangible through his parables and actions. A well-known example of this is the story of the adulteress in the gospel of John (7:53‑8:11): This passage tells of a woman living in adultery.

The scribes drag her to Jesus in order to pass judgment on her. With this demand, they are hoping for an ideal opportunity to find an accusation against Jesus for, since he is known for his merciful treatment of sinners. The scholars are convinced that his mercy will lead him to contradict the Torah: For the Torah commands that an adulterer and an adulteress shall not live (Deut. 20:10). In this scene, however, the male protagonist is missing, who obviously must have been part of the adulterous act. Jesus sees through their deception and does not respond to their unilateral demand: Neither does he violate the Torah by acquitting the woman, nor does he condemn the adulteress. Instead, he chooses a third way to deal with the situation. He moves the audience to self-reflection by saying the famous words: "Let him who is without sin among you be the first to cast a stone at her." (Jn. 8:7) This confronts them with the fact that they have all become guilty and that they could also take the woman's place as the accused. With this realization, the bystanders leave the scene. First the old people, perhaps wiser and more insightful, leave, then all the others. This gesture is tantamount to an admission of guilt. The church father Augustine aptly summarized the point of this story: "Only two remain, the pitiful and the merciful."[3] In the end, Jesus refused to condemn the woman as the other groups in the story hastened to do. He does not even call her to repentance, which may have caused trouble for many believers in church history. She was just to live a holy life from then on.

In this account by the evangelist John, Jesus' mercy and grace are revealed. But the woman is not the only focus of Jesus' action: He keeps the bystanders from doing something wrong and he does not condemn them for their guilt. He makes them reflect on their own lives and deeds and thus shows them his mercy.

What impresses me the most about this story is Jesus' approach, which I consider exemplary and worthy of imitation: Unlike most people, the Son of God apparently does not use a person's guilt to make him compliant.

He also does not pass judgment prematurely. It is in this very case that I have failed so many times in the past. When the issue was clear to me, I succumbed to the temptation to rush to share my insights with all concerned. Jesus, as described in the Gospels, first pauses and takes the time necessary to consider and assess the whole situation. His judgment is not biased or impartial. He considers all those involved. That's what we can learn from Jesus. We will never be completely objective because perfect neutrality cannot be achieved. But it is at least possible for us to act like Jesus and put ourselves in the place of all concerned.

1.4 GRACE IN PAUL

The grace of God plays a very significant role in the life and writings of the apostle Paul. In the years prior to his conversion, he was of the opinion that he could gain value for himself through his achievements – a way of thinking that is perhaps not unfamiliar to us. Formerly known as Saul of Tarsus, his zeal for God's approval turns

---

3   *Augustinus: Des heiligen Kirchenvaters Aurelius Augustinus Vorträge über das Evangelium des hl. Johannes, 111.*

him into a persecutor of Christians. He does not realize that his desire to distinguish himself with the God of Israel makes him his enemy. When the voice of Jesus calls him by name (Acts 9:4f.), he becomes aware of what he has done. Yet the punishment for his actions is not imminent. Instead, he is called to be an apostle, so he must proclaim: "For I am the least of the apostles, unworthy to be called an apostle, because I persecuted the church of God. But by the grace of God I am what I am." (1 Cor. 15:9f.)

Paul experienced God's grace personally and intensely. Through his development from a law-abiding Jew and educated scribe to an apostle and important theologian, a special understanding of grace unfolds in him.

Charis, as it appears in Paul, means more than just a form of mercy, as we will see below. Paul is so moved by God's action toward him and toward humanity that he summarizes his own history (Rom. 1:5; 1 Cor. 15:10; Gal. 1:15; 1 Tim. 1:13f.) and even the entire destiny of humanity under the concept of grace (Rom. 3:21-24): "All" in creation who are lost and separated from God are given access to God through His unique act of grace on the cross. In Jesus, God's grace was revealed and given to us. He brings it into our world, sustains it, and gives it. This is why Paul sometimes refers to *charis* as "the grace of Christ" (e.g., 1 Thess. 5:28; 2 Cor. 8:9; 13:13).

I will now explain this act of God's grace in more detail through the individual aspects that Paul is describing.

THE ORIGINAL DESTINY OF HUMAN BEINGS

At the root and ultimate goal of God's grace with humanity is our original vocation. In my opinion, this vocation is first and foremost love. This statement may seem too short or too simple to some. However, I would like to explain in the following why I believe this: Man was created in the image of God (Gen. 1:26f.; 5:1; 9:6; Col. 3:10; Jas. 3:9). Yet this likeness is not simply a quality that everyone possesses, but a kind of destiny. From the beginning, it was intended and possible for human beings to walk in the love of God and to live filled with it with their fellow human beings and with creation. This potential was given to human beings, and each one of us still possesses it to some degree. It is true that in the past there was often a belief in Christianity that the image of God was the mandate for dominion over creation (Gen 1:26).[4] Perhaps many still hold this belief today. But if we take a closer look at the Bible at this point, we find that the mandate to rule is rather a consequence of the likeness. This does not mean that the image of God is identical with the mandate to rule. Rather, the mandate to rule must be seen in the likeness of God.

It is intended for humans to exercise dominion similar to the loving heavenly Father. God and His Son Jesus Christ are the creators and sustainers of this earth (Col. 1:17), not exploiters and subjugators. Therefore, the purpose of human beings on earth is to pass on the love of God. Furthermore, humans are not only given the mission to rule. Gen. 2:15 tells us that God placed man in the Garden of Eden and instructed them to cultivate and preserve it or to maintain and watch over it. But unfortunately, man is only partially successful in this task. People who recognize this destiny treat creation differently. The following proverb in our vernacular is no accident: "When a farmer is converted, his cattle in the barn also notice." Unfortunately, the Free Church landscape in Germany has not paid much attention to this topic so far.

I would like us to rediscover our responsibility and our role as friends of creation. For this is certain: Our destiny as the image bearers of God is to love one another - but also to care for the world in which we live!

---

4   While in the extra-biblical tradition the king is "the image of God" by virtue of his royal office, in the biblical creation narrative this dignity and this task is assigned to all human beings without distinction. Here, the concept is almost "democratized": Not on the basis of special achievements or tasks, but as human beings they are royal images of God.

Man's rebellion against God disrupts God's good plan for his entire creation. I would like to explore these connections in more detail: The Creator commanded Adam and Eve in the Garden of Eden not to eat of the tree of the knowledge of good and evil. With the prohibition, God also informed them of the consequences that would befall them if they transgressed: They would have to "die of death" (Gen. 2:17). His intention was not to deprive them of the knowledge of good and evil, but to protect them from death and separation from their Creator. For, unlike the animals, God had created man as his counterpart, with whom he now had a desire for relationship. To make real connection and love possible, he also had to give them freedom of choice. However, since freedom also requires meaningful boundaries in order for life and love to be made possible and sustained, God had to communicate His good commandment to Adam and Eve. But human beings always had the choice to say no to this commandment.

To say no was to say no to the One who set the limits, God.

Saying no to God, in turn, also meant rejecting the life He had given. We know the outcome of the event: In spite of everything, the first humans rebelled against God's good limit and acted disobediently. Death, which their Creator had warned them about, did not occur immediately after the Fall. And yet, God did not tell them that they would one day die or become mortal by transgressing His boundaries. This was not an oversight on God's part. The Hebrew phrase used here is typical of threats in prophetic and narrative texts (1 Sam. 14:39; 1 Ki. 2:37; 2 Ki. 1:4).

A parallel passage in 1 Kings 2:36-46 shows the meaning of our expression. Judgment has been passed and its execution will come, though not on the same day. Death, though not immediate, is inevitable. In addition to the physical death, death has now received a "sting" (1 Cor. 15:55). Natural death, which came later, was poisoned because of man's disobedience to God's limit, thus leading to a "second death" (Rev. 2:11), which is eternal separation from God (Rev. 20:6).

The serpent was actively involved in this momentous human transgression. He tempted Adam and Eve to take this step (Gen. 3:1-6): In conversation with the first woman, he first presented God's commandment as an exaggerated demand – as if God had said that one must not eat of *any fruit* in the garden. His desire quickly becomes clear to the reader: He wanted to challenge God's limit. Eve invoked God's command, but she was still engaged in a dialogue with the serpent and his questioning of the Creator's integrity. According to the serpent, God's envy was the reason for his prohibition. He was only concerned that man not become like God. In the end, he succeeded: Adam and Eve finally doubted God's good intentions and broke God's first commandment by eating from the fruit. This was man's first attempt to become like God.

Since then, he has not given up this quest – until today. Modern man also dreams of being his own master. People try to live autonomously and achieve self-realization. This may not be bad in all respects. However, I believe that as creatures we are limited in our wisdom; that there is someone who can guide our lives into good paths that we are not able to recognize on our own. As much as man strives for unlimited self-efficacy, he also longs for immortality. I have the impression that this desire has increased in Western society in recent years. The subject of death is completely ignored, and entire industries profit from this denial. In the meantime, even the technology and Internet companies are devoting themselves to this subject and are looking for a way to make man equal to God by striving to delay the mortality of man.

Thus, with the transgression of God's good commandments, an alienation of man took place, the effects of which continue to this day. Man lives in sin, separate and apart from God, instead of in relationship with Him. This is an existence for which he was not originally intended. It misses the ultimate goal and purpose that God had for man. Living in sin does not simply mean that people keep committing guilty transgressions, although our language suggests this.[5] The word sin is therefore mistakenly equated with guilt. According to the biblical understanding, sin is not simply guilt or a rebellion against God that must have consequences. The meaning of sin is broader; it represents a holistic failure to reach the goal: Man misses the path and destiny that God has intended for him.

But why is this distinction important? God does not use sin to reproach us, to tell us that we always fail and that we should try harder to do everything right.

He wants to tell us: "My children, you are missing the true purpose for which I created you. That goal is love."

CONSEQUENCE OF SEPARATION

In his Epistle to the Romans, the apostle Paul details how the first human being's one failure has led to consequences affecting the entire human race. This has resulted in the entire human race being vulnerable to sin (Rom. 5:12):

Therefore, just as sin came into the world through one man, and death through sin, and so death spread to all men because all sinned.

With this phrase, Paul is not referring to the sinful deeds of each individual that he will eventually commit. He is speaking of a completed process in the past. Through the one sin of the first man, all have become sinners. This idea is confirmed by Paul in the following passage (Rom. 5:13-19). He is particularly clear in verse 18, where he says: "Therefore, as through one man's offense judgment came to all men..."

The sin of which Paul speaks here is not to be understood as a kind of substance inherited by all human descendants. Rather, it is to be

---

5 *When we speak of man's guilty transgressions, we often use the word sin.*

understood as a power that reigns in people and from there spreads its poison. Through it, there exists a state of estrangement from God (caused by the first sin of Adam and Eve) into which every human being is born. Therefore, all people are initially separated from Him and are sinners in the eyes of God. Of course, they remain His creatures whom He loves and seeks. But they are not yet children of God because they are still separated from Him. Sin is the cause of human discord, injustice, and lovelessness. These negative consequences have been with mankind from the beginning.

With all the education, with all the progress and with all the scientific knowledge, no generation has succeeded in eliminating these forces from the world. A glance at the daily newspaper or the news is enough to show that the power of sin is a reality that we will always encounter in this world. This condition in which mankind now exists does not only have a destructive power in life on earth. As mentioned earlier, sin also has a significant impact on death, which thereby receives an additional sting (1 Cor. 15:55): Man remains separated from God even beyond earthly death.

RECONCILIATION THROUGH GRACE

God created a way out of this seemingly hopeless dilemma. He turned to his creatures once again and sent his Son to remove the obstacle. Jesus of Nazareth became man to break the power of sin. Through his death on the cross, mankind has received the greatest grace that can be experienced. This grace is presented in Paul's epistles as the supremacy over sin and wants to be effective in a healing way for all people (Rom. 5:15; Tit. 2:11). Accordingly, God's grace is not limited in time to this life and is not temporary, as was believed in the pagan environment of the apostle Paul. On the contrary, it brings eternal life in the present (Tit. 3:7). For this grace to become a reality in a person's life, the individual's return to a life with God is necessary (Mt. 3:2). In our (Pentecostal) circles we also speak of *conversion* when we speak of such a return. Jesus Christ becomes active in a person's life and moves the person into a life-changing reality. The convert now takes a different path. He no longer acts as he did before. He would not do this on his own, but is now in close fellowship with the living God. In addition, his own goals and thought patterns change. The result of this conversion is the new birth (Jn. 3:3-7). It can be understood as the other side of this reality:

One is conversion, the other is rebirth. The Christian now has a new life. In the Bible believers are also called "new creation" (Gal. 6:15; 2 Cor. 5:17). Of course, through these events man is neither already sinless nor has reached his goal. But although he is not yet in his final form (1 Jn. 3:2), he is also no longer under the power of sin (Rom. 8:9). Julius Schniewind has captured this tension in a play on words: "The Christian is not yet a complete child of God, but he is completely a child of God."[6]

This grace is by its very nature unconditional. It cannot be earned or worked for (Rom. 3:24; 4:4; 11:6; Tit. 3:5). The sovereign and powerful God gives it to man as a free gift (Eph. 2:8f.):

For by grace, you have been saved through faith. And this is not your own doing; it is the gift of God, not a result of works, so that no one may boast.

If you have not yet accepted this gift of grace for yourself personally, I can only advise you to do so. If you – like most of the readers of this book – have already experienced God's grace, I hope that I have been able to give you a good overview of the scope of this gift.

1.5 CONCLUSION

In summary, grace is a loving and free provision of God to humanity. He does not owe us anything and is not dependent on us in any way. Yet He wants to go and be there for us. His grace is inexhaustible and

---

6 *Schniewind: Das biblische Wort von der Bekehrung, 22.*

not limited by time. This gift of God, which transforms our human present and future, is grace in the true sense of the New Testament. Let me give you an example from my family: My wife Irene and I decided a few years ago to take in a young man as our son. He did not work to earn the position, but we both decided to do it. Now he is part of our family. His children are also our grandchildren and are treated and loved as our own offspring, although they are obviously of a different background. Similarly, as children of God, we have become co-heirs with Christ without any action on our part. He has loved and accepted us. Thus we come to enjoy the grace of God.

This explains the essential meaning of grace. What has been explained so far does not cover the full range of the meaning of grace in the New Testament. In the following chapters of this book, however, I will gradually shed light on other aspects of the biblical concept of grace so that it will become clearer and clearer.

❓ QUESTIONS FOR PERSONAL REFLECTION.

1.   Grace is more than a form of mercy. What meaning have you given to the concept of grace in the past?

2.   Grace is unconditional, but it is also not imposed on us. In order for it to become a reality in our lives, we must accept it. Have you already accepted this grace for yourself?

3.   We have been told of man's true destiny, which is to walk in God's love and to pass it on to others and to creation. Where does this purpose come into play in your life?

2 GRACE THAT EMPOWERS

2.1 BE SATISFIED WITH MY GRACE

The grace that God gives us and that makes us a new creation in Jesus Christ and God's children is not just a passive status that we have from now on. It works in believers. Paul tells us that it was reflected in his life as an empowering power and strength.

In the second letter to the Corinthians (12:9) there is a very well-known passage that is often passed on as a consolation when people find themselves in a phase of weakness and brokenness. When this verse is quoted, it is easy to overlook the strength that is actually the subject of the verse:

But he said to me, «My grace is sufficient for you, for my power is made perfect in weakness.» Therefore, I will boast all the more gladly of my weaknesses, so that the power of Christ may rest upon me.

Similarly to Job, the Lord gave the enemy room to work in Paul's life. The attacks to which the apostle was subjected caused him anguish and pain. There are various hypotheses as to what this suffering might have consisted of, but none of them is really certain. Paul asked the Lord three times to deliver him from his suffering. And God heard his prayer and answered it. However, He did not do what the apostle had actually asked Him to do. Instead, He made it clear that these attacks would continue and that Paul needed nothing more than His grace.

In the grace of God, Paul already had everything he needed to persevere in his situation. He needed nothing else, for grace shows its power when man's resources are exhausted. Even more: It is *perfected* in human weakness. God's grace works as an overcoming power especially in those times when we realize that we lack the strength and ability to meet the challenges of life. This realization led Paul to the decision to admit his own weakness and inadequacy in the future in order to benefit all the more from God's grace or power. He turned his eyes from his weaknesses to God's possibilities. The apostle can be a model for us in this as well. Our own inadequacies often lead us to focus on what we cannot do rather than on what is essential. The grace of God helps us to change our focus and turn to more important things.

Let me give you a personal example: For many years I have suffered from various allergies. Despite extensive fasting and praying, I have not been healed of my ailments. I am often asked to stay after my sermons to pray with people, lay hands on them and bless them. I have seen many sick people healed after my prayers. However, I myself have not yet experienced any relief from my ailments. This will probably remain the case, as I suffer from allergies that occur almost exclusively in European vegetation. Since my ancestors left Germany almost three centuries ago, my immune system is probably no longer attuned to the local flora. In the past, I often wondered if it was better to stop praying for the sick. Should I not be healed before I intercede for someone else? In addition, people I had not asked for advice always suspected that there was something wrong in my life. Hidden sin in my private life could very well be the reason why I would not be healed from my suffering. This form of advice felt like a blow.

By now I firmly believe that God does not let us dictate how He should act. He works sovereignly and especially in and through phases of personal weakness.

Nevertheless, in times like these, we like to ask the question *why*. From my point of view, identifying reasons is not very promising because it looks backward. People look for blame and explanations. In such situations, the question *what for* seems more appropriate to me, because challenges and trials usually have a purpose and they can serve us. The question *what* for is thus looking forward and purposeful. James 1:2-4 tells us what such trials are for: They happen so that we can grow personally and become more mature.

Paul's words in 2 Corinthians 12:9 have taught me not to make my emotions the measure of all things, because when it comes to the power and grace of God, they are not always very helpful: our emotions may be genuine. But they can lead us astray, because they are a product of our life experiences and our thoughts. If we change our thinking and have new experiences, the emotions will change as well. But how can this happen? As humans, we tend to look at our own condition. We wonder if we are even worthy of serving God. In doing so, if we focus our eyes on our weaknesses and failures instead of on Jesus Christ, we may feel that we are not good enough. But this is no reason not to dedicate ourselves to the service of our Lord, for it is precisely in our personal inadequacy that the grace of God works. It would be a mistake to withdraw because of our own negative self-image. We see in many places in the New Testament that when God fills a person with His Holy Spirit and sends him out into the world, empowerment follows (e.g. Acts 2:1-4).

2.2 BY GOD`S GRACE I AM WHAT I AM.

Let us look again at the passage from 1 Cor. 15:10, which I mentioned briefly in the first chapter. Upon closer examination, it becomes clear that the apostle Paul also understood grace as an enabling power. Thus, he wrote:

But by the grace of God I am what I am, and His grace toward me was not in vain. On the contrary, I worked harder than any of them, though it was not I, but the grace of God that is with me.

Paul had to realize once again that he could not praise himself for his development - even though he had worked more than any other apostle and had worked powerfully for his Lord: In his ministry he traveled the then-known world and preached the message of the Kingdom of God to many of his contemporaries. He founded new churches, settled disputes, taught, comforted, and encouraged many brothers and sisters in faith. His influence on the beginnings of Christianity cannot be denied. Today, historians say that he was the first theologian to have a decisive influence on European intellectual history. Yet Paul himself emphasized that it was not he who was responsible for these great deeds, but the grace of God that was with him. The enabling power that had led to his accomplishments was not his own, but the efficacy of God's grace. Paul was firmly convinced that he could not have embarked on this path by his own ability, nor could he have passed through it successfully. Even his biography did not seem decisive in the apostle's eyes to become such a formative personality. He reported in Gal. 1:15 that his calling was by God's grace alone (see also 2 Cor. 3:5). Only in this way could he change from a determined persecutor of Christians to a follower of Christ and carry out his blessed ministries. In my ministry, I have often reflected on how much I owe to God's grace and how few of my earlier conditions seemed favorable for God's plan to come to pass for me: I was born and raised in a small town in Kazakhstan as one of eleven children.

My mother had a total of 16 pregnancies, two of which did not end happily. Three of my other siblings died in infancy. Medical care as we know it today did not exist for us. My parents had neither wealth nor did they have the opportunity to enjoy much education as Germans in the Soviet Union. All in all, their life was very hard and arduous. My father was a God-fearing man and a preacher, which brought me many blessings in my younger years, but also put a tremendous strain on my childhood. Belief in a God contradicted the Communist state ideology and this led to Christians being harassed, marginalized, mistreated, and murdered in the Soviet Union. As children, my siblings and I were repeatedly humiliated at school. Teachers would incite the other students against us, sometimes shaming us in front of the class or otherwise intimidating us. The discrimination I experienced in my childhood was not always easy to deal with. I repeatedly had to defend myself or fight for others. One good thing came out of it: I learned to be brave and to stand up for the weak.

My father certainly didn't do everything right in my upbringing. But I am very grateful to him for a lot of things - especially for teaching me to love God and to hold on to the Holy Scriptures. I read the Bible a lot and I gave my life to Jesus Christ at an early age. Accordingly, persecution for of my faith continued into adulthood. Although I did not know the scientific discipline of apologetics[7], I became a kind of defender of Christian doctrine. I read various works of philosophical literature and enjoyed talking about faith on an intellectual level.

During my vocational training, I met a young man whom I told a lot about Jesus. He became open to God and the Christian faith. Unfortunately, he was soon drafted into the Red Army and there killed by the other soldiers because of his profession of Christ. They stabbed his eyes, cut out his tongue, and hanged him. These are memories that are still very painful to me.

After my training as a mechatronics engineer, I was eventually drafted into the Red Army. During my muster, the officers noticed that I was not a party member and a confrontation promptly ensued. My answer to their question of why was simple: «I am a Christian,» I told them. They replied that my faith would be beaten out of me in the army. In the end, their threat was not carried out. Though I was repeatedly scrutinized and had to listen to some lectures, I left the Red Army after two years without any major hostilities. But the pressure I faced as a committed Christian in the army always weighed on me.

With my wife and our own six children, I emigrated to Germany in November 1988. It was a big step for us as a family. We arrived with almost empty hands. There was not much we could take with us from Kazakhstan. We had to learn a new language and make a home in a foreign culture and place. Germans in the Soviet Union were socialized differently than in this country, so it took some time for us to fully arrive here internally. In spite of my efforts to become a part of the local population, I remained a foreigner in the eyes of many, and I am probably still seen as a foreigner to this day.

---

7   Apologetics» is the «defense of Christian truth». Hauck/Schwinge: Theologisches Fach- und Fremdwörterbuch, 21.

At the end of the 1990s, I followed God's call to become a pastor, which I had consistently avoided until then, and began theological training on the side. Due to personal fears, I had never actually imagined going into church ministry, but God obviously had different plans.

I took up my first position as a pastor in 2000 in Nienburg an der Weser, which could not exactly be described as a secure and lucrative job with 33 church members. The congregation organized itself independently and had no major outside resources at its disposal. As a father of six children, this step was more than a gamble for me. But God rewards those who venture into uncertainty by trusting in Him. Abraham is also often called a hero of faith. But what was his heroic act? It was that, trusting God, he took a path to another place that was completely foreign to him (Heb. 11:8). As with Abraham, God has been faithful to me. Even today I look back on the blessed time in Nienburg with joy. In 2009 I moved to a larger congregation in the regional capital of Hanover.

After twelve years of pastoral work, I was elected President of the Federation of Free Churches of Pentecost at the 117th Federal Conference in 2012. What sounds like a glorious moment turned out to be more of a debacle. I did not even receive 52% of the votes of the Federal Conference of pastors and leaders from the individual congregations. This was anything but a clear mandate. My feelings and common sense advised me not to accept this election under any circumstances, because the result could not be described as a clear calling by the assembly. In contrast, however, my values taught me to follow the advice of my leaders: Our former president Ingolf Ellßel told me that he had the impression that I should accept the election. God would bless the time of service. The brothers of the former board expressed the same wish. So I accepted this appointment after all. Serving as president has been a great challenge for me, made more difficult at the beginning by the poor election results. But the new Board stood united with me and gave me strong support. After completing my first five years as president with my strong team, I was reelected by the Federal Assembly in fall 2017.

This time I received a clear mandate from my brothers and sisters. When I first entered a Pentecostal church as a young Baptist, 35 years prior to this, I would not have dared to dream of the ways the Lord would prepare for me in the future.

But why am I writing all this? It is not at all my intention to emphasize my person or my life. As already indicated at the beginning, I only want to make clear that the grace of God has also worked abundantly in my life. Together with Paul I can say «by God's grace I am what I am.» The basic conditions for becoming an influential person in this country were very bad for me. My parents lived through famine and prison. They did not teach me to dream big or anything like that. But from a very early age, I had the feeling that God was always with me. I knew that he would give me success if I acted according to his will. This has been confirmed consistently in my life. I believe that our biography only plays a limited role in being of use to God. His grace is able to enable us to do the work to which He has called and ordained us. We cannot choose all the conditions in life. Many circumstances are our own responsibility. But there are unplanned things that happen. Sometimes we are not able to prevent what happens *to us*, but we can influence what happens *in us*. If we look at our curriculum vitae, which is quite common practice in this country, we may quickly be tempted to question our suitability. I would advise against this. It is not always useful to look at one's past. Another mistake we like to make as human beings is to measure ourselves against others. This quote stems from philosopher Sören Kierkegaard, «All adversity comes from comparison.» It may sometimes be useful to look at the gifts and accomplishments of others in order to properly evaluate oneself.

However, we tend to compare apples with oranges. As human beings, we are not able to have an adequate overview of the reality of life, origin, socialization, resources, etc. of our fellow human beings. In this respect, we cannot really make fair comparisons. Each of us is unique with his or her own history. Therefore, a simple comparison is not useful at all – especially if we start to judge. We can leave that to the One who is able to look into all the nooks and crannies of our development and present life. Comparisons generate competition and rivalry. In the pursuit of laurels, there will always be perceived losers. Yet people are often neither worse nor better, just different.

The Bible speaks clearly about all people being equal before God (2 Chr. 19:7; Rom. 2:11; Jas. 2:1-9). These statements are made in a judicial context, and it becomes clear that the Creator makes no distinctions in His judgment of us humans. Our judicial system also prides itself on judging in this way. The Roman goddess Justitia is considered a symbol of justice and adorns many German courtrooms and town halls. Her eyes are blindfolded while she holds the scales in her hand. Like her, our legal system is blind when it comes to the individual. But while Justitia can only judge the bare facts of the case, God looks deeper. «A man looks on the outward appearance, but the LORD looks at the heart.» (1 Sam. 16:7) The Creator considers all the details of our lives and souls. Not only are we all equally valuable and loved in God's eyes, but we can also count on His judgment of us to always be just. At the same time, we can count on the fact that he has only good things in store for us. He does not want to «ruin» us, but to raise us up. His grace is sufficient for all and he desires its power to be effective in our lives. His grace is unconditional, but it does not remain without consequences.

Grace is more visible in some people's lives than in others, because some people seem to claim it more than others. The reasons may vary, but I know that for some it is because of the belief that they have to perform. Personally, I have struggled with accepting gifts myself in the past. For some reason I believed I would have to return them one day or make a return payment for them. I felt in the interpersonal area of my life as I felt in the area of faith: I found it difficult to accept God's grace as a gift with all its implications. Some readers may feel similarly.

I certainly believe that little children can show us a way in this: At our family Christmas, I love watching our grandchildren. They often know ahead of time what gifts they are going to get. But when they receive the ones they want, their eyes are full of excitement and they accept them without hesitation. In my spiritual life I have also learned to become like a child (Mt. 18:3) and accept God's grace. God's grace is abundant for everyone, but there is still a considerable number of believers who do not allow it to be effective. I am convinced that divine empowerment cannot be fully developed in a person's life as long as he remains passive. It is up to us to embrace and allow the grace of God. In the following part I will explain how this is possible.

❓ Questions for personal reflection.

1. God's grace does not remain ineffective in us, but past experiences are easily forgotten. Where has God's grace been formative and empowering in your life?

2. Has the enabling grace of God come to fruition in you? If not, what could be the cause?

3. Read 2 Timothy 2:1. Could Paul's invitation to his disciple also be an invitation to you?

Part 2:
Accepting
God`s grace

3   THE MEASURE OF GRACE

As I am writing this book, my main activity is to preside over the Pentecostal movement in Germany. Visits to churches and theological training centers in Germany and many other countries are also on my agenda. I accompany and advise leaders and congregations in various issues and processes. My range of tasks is complex. I often feel very challenged, but all in all, I gratefully accept this stage of my life from God's hand. Since my term as president is limited, I am often asked what my plans are for the future.

Unfortunately, I cannot answer this question, which surprises many of the people I talk to. In my opinion, this decision is not mine alone. Just because I like to do something or have experience in it does not mean that the Lord will give me the necessary grace to do it. For this stage of my life and my current tasks, I have received everything I need from God to master the challenges involved. When this time is over, I will receive new assignments from the Lord, which He will prepare. I recognize that such thoughts are not new to most Christians. Yet they may seem strange to some of us, for why not go back to doing something we already know how to do in the future? Why go into uncharted territory all over again? Why give up on something that works?

3.1 A PERSON CANNOT TAKE ANYTHING

Surrender and grace - these two aspects don't seem to go together at first glance. Or do they? I have written before about my conviction that God, by His grace, enables people to serve in spite of the most adverse circumstances. Such a view may be more familiar to us Christians.

But God's grace can be effective not only in perseverance and holding on, but also in giving up, in letting go. The crucial question is: Where does God's path lead? I therefore believe that it is just as important to let go when the time is right. Otherwise we are in danger of blocking new developments. Sadly, I often see people not only hindering progress, but holding onto what exists until what remains is completely broken. There are countless attempts to pour old wine into new wineskins. But we know from our Lord that this is not a good idea.

Sure, letting go is not always easy. Often the previous activity gives us a certain identity. This can be lost on the way to new shores. Leaving the known and the familiar can also mean getting involved in uncertainties and losing influence. As we age, it becomes increasingly difficult to let go and embrace the new because, as we know, you don't replant an old tree. But life is in permanent flux and our roles are constantly changing. This is also true within the family: In the mature years of my life, my role as a father to my children has changed a lot. I have become their friend. It would be strange for me to talk to them and make demands the way I used to. If I did, they would probably interact with me less. I help where I can and give advice from time to time when asked.

A biblical example of how to healthily let go and release God's grace to ourselves and others is found in Moses and Joshua. Joshua accompanied Moses, learned from him, experienced God in a special way during this time together, and realized what Israel owed to God. Eventually he was given the position of his teacher. It is sad to say that Joshua did not follow Moses' example. He did not find a successor and the consequences were devastating. The generation that followed Joshua's generation was alienated from the God of Israel and they abandoned Him (Jdg. 2:7-13).

We can learn from this story and be aware that there will be a time after we pass the baton. We want not only to be doers, but also to set the course for others. Above all, we want to pass the baton promptly when the time comes.

The fact that people do not let go at the right time is not only problematic because they may block further development. They also often get in their own way. Certainly, those who are successful in life are those who remain stubborn and persistent and do not allow themselves to be diverted from their goals. But there is also a healthy form of surrender when the goals set are unrealistic and do not bring the expected success.

   The measure of grace

For us as believers, there is another perspective on why surrender can sometimes be the better path: Scripture teaches us that the success of our actions is not simply determined by the classic factors of perseverance, talent, and willingness to suffer, but ultimately depends on another crucial factor: Let's look at some New Testament passages for this purpose. John 3:22 begins by describing the conflict between those following Jesus and those following John the Baptist. Disturbed by Jesus' actions, the disciples of John seek out their master. A conversation ensued in which they told him that they had observed Jesus baptizing in the same region as their Master, but that his baptism differed in some respects from the customs of Jesus. Perhaps the community of John practiced additional purification rites that were not used by Jesus – the exact situation is unknown to us. What is certain is that the disciples of John apparently viewed these different practices of Jesus and his missionary success as a questionable competition in the same region. The text at least conveys the feeling that a certain envy resonates in their question: And they came to John and said to him, "Rabbi, he who was with you across the Jordan, to whom you bore witness – look, he is baptizing, and all are going to him." (3:26) Johns' answers in verse 27 is a principle:

A person cannot receive even one thing unless it is given to him from heaven.

The master makes it clear to his followers that Jesus' success is due to God's work. This other rabbi would not have had the power to attract so many people on his own if he had not been given power from above.
The Baptist's statement also teaches us that spiritual life cannot be produced at will. God's kingdom is always present in His church, but it never completely passes into their hands, because it is His kingdom. It is and remains dependent on Him and His grace (cf. also Jn. 15:5).

Part 2: Accepting God`s grace | 39

We must not always attribute failures and setbacks to a lack of God's favor: For as long as we are in this world, we also remain subject to its adversities and there are numerous other reasons for failure. Even so, the principle already mentioned that a man cannot take anything unless it is given to him from heaven (Jn. 3:27) still applies. In this context, some may also recall the old German proverb that says: "Everything depends on God's blessing." This popular saying probably originated from the interpretation of Psalm 127. It describes that all human efforts are in vain if God does not cooperate (Ps. 127:1f.). However old and well-known the proverb may be, it still seems to be forgotten time and again. I have benefited from it many times because on the one hand it reminds me that we are not alone - which is a relief; on the other hand it helps me to be vigilant and to check if I feel God's anointing in the ministry I am doing. Otherwise, it would be wiser to leave the ways in which God does not work with me and through me. If he is not with me, I labor in vain. A work that God does not bless becomes tedious and burdensome. It lacks the grace that is necessary.

Nobody wants to get worn out serving without God's enabling grace. But how do we know the right time to let go? I am often asked this question. I think that our role in life and our education is like the flow of life itself: Our environment is in permanent flux, so our role should also never become static and our education never complete. And when I speak of education, I do not mean training in the sense of adapting to a given market. It is not a matter of being tailored to a specific field of activity by means of training, but rather of continuing to develop and grow in a permanent and holistic way. A person who faces this process and allows himself to be guided by the Holy Spirit will recognize the right time and be ready for the next task that the Lord gives him.

When I was younger, I dreamed of being a retired pastor at 60 and planting churches instead. I made plans for my future. Blaise Pascal is said to have said: "If you want to make God laugh, tell him about your plans." I probably made my Creator smile a little too, because He had other plans for my life: A few years ago, I was given the grace to be a mentor and promoter of young men. I have taken this sphere of action from God's hand. My spiritual sons are now the ones who found the churches. Of course, as a mentor and advisor I no longer take as much priority and they carry of the laurels. I am not sad about that. After all, it is not about me personally, but about the work of Jesus Christ, and my dream of planting churches has been fulfilled, albeit in a different way.

3.2 MANIFOLD GRACE

It is good for people to serve in what they have been given, and with the realization that a person cannot take anything beyond that, we now return to the concept of grace. As we look further into the New Testament, we see that the enabling grace we have been looking at is not always of the same kind. It exists in many forms. Paul, for example, according to his own testimony, was given a very special kind of grace. Thus, he legitimizes his instructions to the Romans with this very grace given to him (Rom. 12:3), which he also mentions again elsewhere (1 Cor. 3:10; Gal. 2:9, Eph. 3:7). Furthermore, the apostle speaks of the fact that the Lord gives everyone a certain *measure* of grace. Unlike his opponents, he does not boast endlessly, but according to the measure given to him (2 Cor. 10:13-15). In Romans 12:3, Paul also admonishes the believers not to think of themselves more highly than they ought, but to keep within the measure that God has given each one. Paul writes similarly and even more clearly in Eph. 4:7:

But grace was given to each of us according to the measure of Christ`s gift.

The congregational context clearly indicates that we are talking about a grace that serves the building up of the church (and obviously not the grace of salvation). Finally, in verse 11, Paul comes to talk about the various ministries, which we will cover at a later time. From my point of view, the certain measure of grace cannot be limited to this group of people alone, but in verse 7 all of Christianity is addressed. Each of the believers is given a certain share of grace. The task of the ministries is now to develop this part in the brothers and sisters so that it becomes effective.

But what exactly does Paul mean when he speaks of this "measure of grace"?

The assumption that this is about a certain spectrum of gifts (in the sense of charisms) is, in my view, too narrow, since the term charisms does not appear once in the letter. So we would be doing the text a disservice if we reduced it to the gifts alone. The gifts, which we will discuss in detail in the later part of this book, are also to be understood more as tools. Grace on the other hand encompasses much more. It is, as I have explained in chapter 2, a special ability, a power that shapes the character of man and, according to Paul's statements, is given differently to each believer. Peter also tells us something similar when he speaks of the "manifold" grace (1 Pet. 4:10).

As each one has received a gift, use it to serve one another, as good stewards of God`s varied grace.

God's grace, according to Peter, is not uniform or monotonous, but manifests itself differently in each person.[9] Not every believer is given the same grace.

What I am presenting here based on the Bible is something that most people have probably already observed in their environment or in their own lives. The spheres of activity, spheres of influence, spheres of responsibility and aptitudes of believers are very different. This in itself makes sense and would not be problematic if we as humans did not tend to judge. The great, the special or the superlative have always fascinated us. In that sense some forms of grace

---

9 *Grace can also be rendered as «colorful» because the word poikilos that Peter uses here also means «multicolored.»*

seem to be very special and significant, while others seem rather uninteresting and trivial. For the most part it is precisely what I do not have that is interesting and desirable, while what is mine has already lost its appeal. When my grandchildren hold a toy in their hands that is actually intact and brings them joy, they are satisfied until they see one of their siblings with a supposedly better toy that they don't have.

Before long, a special sense of justice is developed, and the demands are not long in coming. As adults we may smile at this behavior, but ultimately, we are very similar to children: We devalue our own because we believe that the other's is more valuable.

I am often asked why God distributes His grace so differently. "Have others perhaps earned or worked for something with God?" "Do some enjoy certain privileges?" "Is God unfair?" My answer to these questions is usually short and simple: God distributes differently, because we humans are different. Everyone is an individual in their own way, unique in their socialization, biography, habits, and circumstances.

It is true that all people have a gift that is not of spiritual nature: It is the ability to learn everything and to adapt to the influences of the environment. This is certainly true, especially for children. For adults, however, this is somewhat different. Of course, even at an advanced age it is still possible to learn a great deal, but the necessary resources are not always available. Time is often more limited and there are often other complicating factors such as social responsibilities to family and loved ones, financial challenges, and lack of motivation. In all of this it is important to keep in mind that mere skills in an area are not always enough to be successful. Even if someone is highly trained theologically, it does not mean that they are resilient, communicative, and persuasive. But these are precisely the qualities needed e.g. for a leadership position in the church. My point is that a person has the ability to learn anything, but only in certain time frames and to a certain degree. Thus, some tasks would simply overwhelm some people, even though they may possess the necessary skills. In addition, a certain degree of grace also brings new circumstances that must be overcome.

More responsibility means, among other things, more conflict, a greater commitment of time, and therefore more stress. It is also important to be prepared for these circumstances.

Many sailors aspire to be captains, but the job requires a wide range of skills and knowledge. Unlike a ship's mechanic, a ship's commander is not only responsible for a few areas, but must have an overview of the whole and be accountable for everything. His knowledge is not limited to shipping. For example, he should also be well versed in legal matters. There are also differences in the size of the watercraft. The responsibilities, workload and areas of knowledge required increase with the size of the ship. When a ship's mechanic is at sea and everything is running smoothly, he may conclude that he can replace the captain's position with his own experience. If he is allowed to take over the position of his commander, which is not very likely, disillusionment would quickly spread to the person in question in the face of unexpected difficulties.

As absurd as such a case of overconfidence may seem in shipping, this phenomenon is, however, common in the church of Jesus Christ: blessed brothers and sisters build up their church community or a regional ministry together over a period of years. The success is probably initially due to the fact that God has given the leader of this work a special grace and blesses him. Among his co-workers, however, are some who are convinced that this success is largely due to their competence. At some point, it is time for the person in charge to vacate the area of authority. It can often be due to changes in age or life circumstances. However, it is not uncommon for a leader to be ousted by his or her team or individual employees.

It may be that disputes and personal disappointments have exhausted the relationships and a new team constellation is needed to remedy the situation. But simple power issues may also be at the root of this situation.

This is why a new leader is being sought. I often see those who have been on the team longer and feel they have made a special contribution to the success of the work in the past start to push themselves to the front. Frequently there are also those people who have not made a special contribution in the past, but who are quite confident in themselves. If God truly gives these people a guiding role, the work will be blessed. But unfortunately, this is not always the case. Often "sailors" overestimate themselves and try to be the "captain." In many cases, however, the success of the work quickly begins to crumble and, over time, they lose the support of their employees. Eventually, they withdraw in disillusionment and disappointment.

If we look at the parable of the entrusted talents in the gospel of Matthew 25:14-30, the above described becomes a little clearer: The narrative begins with a master handing over part of his property to his servants. They are appointed by him over his property, and of course they are now to serve as stewards. The sums entrusted to these servants are large. The daily wage of an unskilled laborer at that time was about one denarius (Mt. 20:1-5). It is believed that one talent was equivalent to about 6,000-10,000 denarii. So even the "little" that the Lord hands over to his servants (Mt. 25:23) is a considerable sum.

Verse 15 describes why the Lord distributed his wealth differently to these servants:

And to one he gave five talents, to another two, and to another one, to each according to his own ability; and immediately he went on a journey.

This parable has been interpreted very differently throughout church history. The interpreters of Scripture have never been able to agree on what exactly these talents mean in a figurative sense.

And it is still a matter of dispute which parts of this parable are actually to be understood as symbolic and which parts merely serve as a narrative framework. A very common interpretation refers to the talents as the gifts that God has given to each person. Whatever these talents consist of, it becomes clear that the master distributes his capital differently because he does not want to overburden the abilities of the servants. He gives to each according to his "strength" or according to his "ability," tailoring the task in some way to the person. Our Lord, who is represented in the parable by the master of the servants, does not burden anyone with more than he can bear, so that no one is overburdened (cf. also 1 Cor. 10:13). This must be understood and accepted. God does not favor and is not unfair, but he is interested in our welfare and success. He, who went to the cross for us so that we might have life, will challenge, form, and shape us. But in all this, our Creator knows the right measure. Sometimes, however, we overwhelm ourselves by setting high expectations for ourselves. But it may also be others who impose too great a burden on us. In all of this, we must keep in mind that we are not disappointing people, but only their personal expectations of us. Our calling is not to please everyone. We are chosen to fulfill the mission the Lord has personally given us.

In the church context, especially in light of this parable, we are reminded again and again that God cares about our faithfulness (v. 23). The question is, what does this faithfulness consist of? It should, of course, be expressed in the wise stewardship of God's talents, not in burying them. But it is precisely the latter that is often the case. In my opinion, this burying does not necessarily happen only because people are passive, even though the parable seems to suggest that at first glance. It also happens when we try to manage talents that have not been entrusted to us, rather than devoting ourselves to what we have. In the following chapter we will explore the details of what this means.

1. Holding on is not always beneficial, and there is also a healthy way to let go. Are there areas in your life or ministry that the Holy Spirit is telling you to let go of in order to embrace the new?

2. We humans tend to evaluate. Are you familiar with grading systems for ministry or spirituality from your own environment or thinking?

3. How have you assessed your own gifts, abilities and strengths? Is there a need to rethink them?

4 Recognizing God`s grace

4.1 Why wanting a lot is not always good

During his lifetime, famous American football coach Vincent "Vince" Lombardi used to say: "Winners never quit and people who quit never win." In saying this, he may have struck at the heart of a widespread pattern of thought in Western culture. In our culture, we are encouraged to strive for greatness, to follow our hearts, and to let nothing stand in the way of our dreams. The virtue of humility and the ability to let go, on the other hand, has no place in our society. Giving up is frowned upon even in pious circles. But is this way of thinking always wise? What if our desires and dreams are not only excessive and unrealistic, but also exceed the measure of our own grace? What are the consequences of this attitude and these false objectives?

In the last chapter I explained that a person cannot take anything unless it has been given to him from heaven. The same is true of grace as it is described in the New Testament: It is bestowed and cannot be bought or earned by us human beings. We can seek, find, and take hold of what God has for us. However, hard work and all our efforts will not lead to success if we take what is not given to us. This dilemma always reminds me of 1 Pet. 4:15:

But let none of you suffer as a murderer or a thief or an evildoer or as a meddler.

The young Christians whom Peter is trying to encourage in this passage suffered persecution and affliction. But as long as they endured these for the sake of their Lord Jesus Christ, they were to be counted as blessed (v. 14). But no Christian should torment himself by being a murderer, thief, criminal, or meddler in other people's affairs. The word that Peter uses here at the end of his list is unique in the Bible and also foreign to the ancient literature of the first century. It is probably most commonly understood in the sense of "busybody" or "intruder". Literally translated the expression means "bishop over strangers." It obviously refers to a person who interferes in the affairs of others. No Christian should suffer for being such a person. I find it remarkable that Peter associates such overstepping of authority with pain. Instead of simply mentioning that such behavior is not proper for a Christian, he briefly and succinctly states the consequences of pomposity: It means personal suffering for the cobbler who does not stick to his last.

I am convinced that people who try to take what the Lord has not given them will experience tribulation in various forms. This can manifest itself as stress, disappointment, overload, failure, and brokenness - just to name a few patterns. In addition, the church of Jesus is also inevitably affected when its members do not remain in the place God has assigned to them.

Through my traveling ministry and consulting work, I often witness power plays in churches. Unfortunately, competition does not always stimulate business. It can also lead to war, and as we know, wars only produce losers, not winners. Churches are worn down or, in the worst case, torn apart by this internal strife. This is not only detrimental to the Body of Christ itself, but it is also detrimental to the gospel, because our fellow human beings, with whom we share the message of love and forgiveness, see when dispute and ill will spread in our churches. Christians, unfortunately, seem to be the only breed of sheep that bites each other. There should be no competition and rank battles in the church of God. Many conflicts and petty wars could be prevented if everyone would only seek what God has given them instead of interfering with strangers.

In the same way, I think many disputes and conflicts could be avoided in the first place, and the churches would also be stronger and more influential. This admonition does not only apply to those who usurp ministry. Leaders also have a responsibility to give others their rightful place and not to keep spheres of influence to themselves. Therefore, my motto is not simply, "I will allow addition." It is rather: "I actively seek complement."

We ourselves are responsible for recognizing our God-given measure and remaining within it. Paul increasingly called on his brothers and sisters in faith to assess themselves correctly. So there were probably brothers and sisters in Roman Christian circles who needed to be reminded not to think of themselves as too important:

For by the grace given to me I say to everyone among you not to think of himself more highly than he ought to think, but to think with sober judgement, each according to the measure of faith that God has assigned. (Rom. 12:3)

The apostle speaks of sobriety in self-evaluation. What the exact background of his words were at that moment is uncertain, but it can be assumed that there were personalities in his environment who were striving for more than was their place. Another passage in which Paul encourages his readers to remain moderate is 1 Cor. 7:17:

Only, let each person lead the life that the Lord has assigned to him, and to which God has called him. This is my rule in all the churches.

The saving grace of God which makes us his children, does not eliminate the great diversity among people. So everyone should be free to live his life as God has intended for him. In the previous verses Paul gives advice to people who have an unbelieving partner (1 Cor. 7:12-16). However, while this advice reflects his opinion, he makes it clear that each person is ultimately responsible for discerning and carrying out God's calling on his or her life. Norbert Baumert aptly reformulates Paul`s words here: "You have to consider my advice yourself and check before God whether it applies in your case.

And this principle always applies!"[10] Even the wise counsel of the apostles is not irrevocable when it comes to what the Lord has assigned to a person. Therefore, each one is challenged to always seek God's counsel for his life. This search should never be completed, because life and our tasks in it are subject to constant change: Man is always entering and completing new stages of development. They come and pass. The search for one's own measure of grace is thus like a journey on which the course needs to be checked and correct-

____

10 Baumert: Sorgen des Seelsorgers, 101. 56

ed again and again. In this way we will certainly reach our goal and avoid going astray.

4.2 LESS IS NOT ALWAYS MORE

The church of Christ does not only suffer from the fact that its members sometimes want more than the Lord has given them. There is probably a much larger number of people who do not grasp their own measure of grace at all. Perhaps they do not want to make mistakes or they fear failure. Or they may believe that they are insignificant. Some may simply be unaware that God needs them. He could of course do His work without us, but He wants to collaborate with us. A closer look at the Bible shows that God often uses natural means, but probably most often He uses human help. When Paul exhorts us not to think too much of ourselves in Romans 12:3, he is surely also exhorting us not to think too little of ourselves. After all, everyone should live as God has measured out to him (1 Cor. 7:17; Eph. 4:7). False modesty is out of place here. We are very important to God. In John 3:16 Jesus reveals how valuable we are to the Creator: God did not even spare His own Son in order to enable mankind to have fellowship with Him again.

4.3 RECONCILING WITH ONE`S OWN MEASURE

I encourage the group of the hesitant and the doubters as much as I encourage the boisterous ones to come to terms with the measure of grace that God has given them and to accept it.
This does not always seem attractive to us at first glance. It may not even correspond to our ideas and desires or it may harm our ego. I have some good news for the disappointed. The New Testament also emphasizes the growing in grace. We will take another look at this subject at the end of this book. But firstly, it is necessary to accept the grace of the Lord. In doing so, we can also accept our own limitations. They are a natural part of us. Not everyone succeeds in everything and this is not a tragedy. In our modern times, some

people like to think of themselves as all-rounders – I like to call such a person a "jack of all trades". However, creatures that can do everything neither exist in nature nor in the human species. The opposite is more likely to be the case: With the increasing complexity of our society and the environment in general, trying to do everything is ultimately an overreach. The most at risk are the meticulous among us. Being perfect and working perfectly costs enormous amounts of energy and resources. Our Lord is not at all concerned with flawless performance. He is concerned first and foremost with the relationship of the heart.

I did not always want to admit my own limitations. A while back, I was asked in a conversation what I thought was my biggest mistake as a leader so far. I believe that it was based on my false assumption that the people around me would change as a result of my presence and the time that I spent with them. So I surrounded myself with people who were supposed to change for the better in my presence. But it did not happen as I had imagined. Instead of being changed, they had a negative influence on me. It was arrogant to think that I would be so influential and persuasive.

I have come to terms with the fact that this assumption was very wrong and I had to pay a high price for it. The Lord is the beginner and perfector of our faith (Heb. 12:2) and His presence changes people. To think that I could do this on my own was simply to overestimate myself, and I had to go back to the measure that had been given to me. As I mentioned earlier, I believe that God is not unfair in the distribution of His grace. Instead, he is interested in our welfare and in the success of our work. When I criticize his measure of me I question the one who measured it. The original sin of man was precisely that he wanted to be like God (cf. chap. 1). He wanted to be his own lord. This inherent human need is still present and is a driving force in the shaping of our lives that we should keep in mind. For such a desire must not be our motivation in seeking our measure of grace.

4.4 RECONGNIZING YOUR OWN MEASURE

It has probably become clear enough by now why it is so important for each person to keep to his or her proper, God-given measure. But perhaps even more uncertainty has arisen within us as to whether the path we have chosen is the right one. It is always a healthy habit to examine ourselves and our ministry from time to time. We should not cease to measure ourselves against the Scriptures and the example of our Lord and to be corrected by them. How do we know that we are moving within the bounds of our own measure and that we have not taken a wrong turn?

Once again, Paul serves as our example. In Galatians 2:1-10 he recounts his meeting with the other apostles who led the early church in Jerusalem. About 14 years after he had visited the city for personal reasons, he was there again. This time he did not enter the city alone, but with a delegation to deal with serious problems.

The disagreement revolved around the mission to the Gentiles that Paul had been promoting for several years, and about which the Jerusalem believers had a different view. Not every exchange of views during his stay led to a consensus. Paul even called some of them "false brothers" who wanted to make the believers slaves of the law again. Apparently, this group of people demanded a Christianity within Judaism. But despite differences of opinion, they were able to come to terms with the supporting "pillars" of the community there. They came to an agreement that James, Peter, and John would continue to work among the Jews, while Paul and his companions would go back to work in the Gentile world. In Gal. 2:9 Paul tells us what led to this decision by the three leading apostles:

And when James and Cephas and John, who seemed to be pillars, perceived the grace that was given to me, they gave the right hand of fellowship to Barnabas and me, that we should go to the Gentiles and they to the circumcised.

The other three apostles noticed the divine anointing that had been given to Paul and agreed to go along with the delegation. The grace to function as a Gentile apostle was visible to the Spirit-filled leaders of that church. Like the situation in New Testament times, grace is present today. When God gives a special grace and it becomes effective, it is also visible to others. Even if it is only a glimmer at the beginning (2 Tim. 1:6), I believe that it becomes more and more evident to our brothers and sisters over time. Therefore, other leaders should also be able to testify to this grace. It is not enough for us alone to be convinced that we have received it. Although I do not always seem to be gifted, and my first election as president went badly, the other leaders on the board have always confirmed God's call for me.

Other leaders saw God's grace for this position relatively early on, but I still had to develop it because much of it was uncharted territory for me. I have followed the same principle all my life:

I only believed that the Lord's grace was given to me after other leaders had confirmed it. Furthermore, I did not actively seek ministry. Rather, I simply responded to the call of mature spiritual leaders who recognized my potential. They recognized God's grace and recommended me – and where God's grace is at work, the fruit of it is soon visible to others.

For most of the tasks that I have taken on, I have had to reinvent myself, and I would like to emphasize that once again in this context: God works with people, not without them. He gives us His grace to do it. And yet we must not believe that everything will come naturally. There is also much to work hard for. For the tasks God has given me, I have acquired literature and sought mentors who have accompanied me on these new paths. God's grace is given to us, but it is up to us to do something with it. In the parable of the vine in John's gospel, Jesus clearly emphasizes that although his disciples can do nothing without him, bearing fruit in this passage is described as an active act:

*I am the vine, you are the branches. Whoever abides in me and
I in him, he it is that bears much fruit, for apart from me you
can do nothing. (Jn. 15:5)*

The call to the disciples is not to sink into contemplation or to warm
the pew, but to bear abundant fruit. The advice to abide in grace is
not given as an end in itself. The goal is to be able to act. And not
from one's own ability, but from the power of communion with the
Lord. It becomes clear that it is man's task to bear fruit in Christ.
Grace, then, has two sides: On the one hand, it is a gift from God,
but on the other hand, it is also a task for man.

This grace becomes visible to others, mature brothers and sisters,
when it becomes effective. However, this does not clarify the works
with which we should begin. Therefore, brothers and sisters often
ask me how they can recognize their personal measure of grace. I
gladly pass on my personal conviction: Take what God puts before
your feet and grow in it! When the Lord calls and equips us, His
mission is not far away. He creates possibilities so that we can grasp
our own measure of grace.

To aid the reader's search (among other reasons), the third part of
this book will discuss the natural gifts, the gifts of the Holy Spirit,
and the fivefold ministry. In doing so, I want to show how the grace
of God works in the life of the believer. I hope that some of you will
be able to discern your own personal measure of grace as you read
this section. Finally, we always have the option of asking God for
wisdom in this matter. In James 1:5 we can read that He gives practical wisdom without reservation to the one who asks for it.

1. Were you aware that you have your own measure of grace? If yes, do you think you have assessed it properly?

2. Everyone has experienced failure at one time or another because it is part of human development. How did spirit-filled brothers and sisters evaluate your failures? Did you take their advice?

3. What is the reaction of your church to your current ministry? Do you receive encouragement and support or are people reluctant to give you feedback?

Part 3:
Serving in the grace of God

5   The work of the Holy Spirit in us

Many Christians are very enthusiastic when they find out that the Holy Spirit wants to work through them – and rightly so! But before we now turn to the gifts and the work of the Holy Spirit, I would like to address a fundamental issue that is of enormous importance for spiritual ministry: God does not only want to work *through* people, but *in* them!

As we have already experienced, His grace does not remain without noticeable effects. God's love shapes and changes us. Sure – He accepts us as we are when we come to Him. But He loves us too much to leave us at that. But do we really want these changes? This question is usually quickly answered in the affirmative. In doing so we may forget that this is a transformation of our personality. However, our own nature is not as easy to change as we think. And in my experience, many people are enthusiastic about change when it does not affect them. I was once asked by a Russian journalist in St. Petersburg what I thought was the greatest miracle of God. I told him that – apart from the salvation of mankind – the most amazing thing for me was the transformation of the personality of the individual. I know from the lives of others, as well as from my own, how difficult it is to work on oneself. But I am convinced that it is necessary if we are to serve in the grace of God in a healthy way. Everyone talks about character – but what is it really? By the word *character* we refer (in a broad sense) to the qualities, attitudes, and behaviors of a person. In short, it includes everything that makes up the personality – that is, what is «characteristic» about it.

However, the term character originally comes from the Greek and refers to a stamp used for minting coins. In this respect a coin became valuable not simply through the metal, but through its minting. In a figurative sense, people are not distinguished by their appearance, but by their character. The actual value of a one-euro coin, including material and production costs, etc., is about 10 cents. The value of the coin is multiplied tenfold by its minting. I like to use this metaphor to describe the importance of the imprint of the Holy Spirit on our character. When the Spirit of God shapes us, our value to the world around us increases many times over.

It fascinates me that God is not particularly interested in the outward appearance. Rather, He looks at the inside of a person. He looks at the heart and that is what He is interested in (1 Sam. 16:7).[11] God wants to shape and form this inner being through His Holy Spirit. In his letter to the Galatians the apostle Paul speaks of the «walk in the Spirit» and «leadership of the Spirit» (Gal. 5:16). The result of such a lifestyle is the «fruit of the Spirit» and Paul lists nine divine qualities: love, joy, peace, patience, kindness, goodness, faithfulness, gentleness, and self-control (Gal. 5:22). Some biblical commentators also refer to these qualities as the character of Jesus Christ – in my opinion rightly so. For if there was ever a human being who embodied these qualities perfectly, it was our Lord Jesus Christ. No one else could make such a statement about themselves.

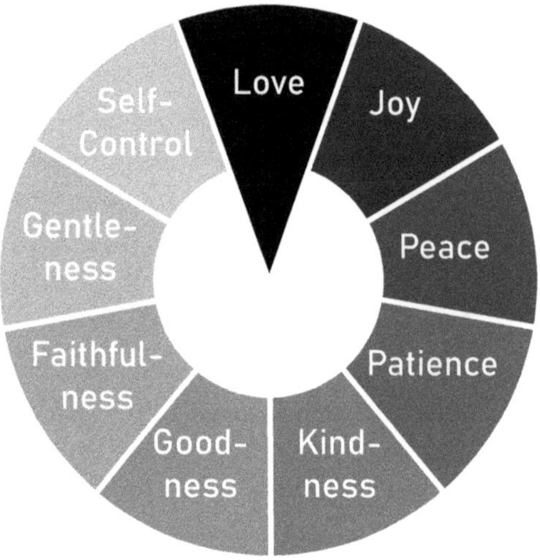

A fruit on a fruit tree, for example, undergoes development and ripening rather than merely existing. Plants go through growth pro-

---

11 *According to Old Testament understanding, the heart refers to the core of man, with which man feels and thinks. As Europeans, we would probably equate the heart with the soul and the mind.*

cesses. In this respect, we human beings are no different from them. Taking steps in the development of character and personality also takes time and requires certain processes. As residents of a wealthy country, we are accustomed to having our needs met quickly. We are reluctant to wait in a crowded restaurant or stand in a long line at the grocery store. Because we rarely practice waiting in line, we simply lack the patience to do so. However, personality change does not happen at the push of a button. Inner processes take time and are certainly not a walk in the park.

A Chinese poem states:

«Money can buy a house, but not a home;
can buy a bed, but not sleep;
can buy a clock, but not time;
can buy a book, but not knowledge...»

I would add: «You can buy outer beauty, but you can't buy character.» Character is formed and shaped. This process is rarely comfortable and quick.

The philosopher Plato was one of the first thinkers to study human development. In his work *Politeia* we find the famous allegory of the cave: A person is trapped in a crevice in a rock. Bound in the world of appearances, the person can only see the shadows of the real things that are projected on the wall. At some point, however, the person succeeds in freeing himself, climbing out of the hole, and seeing the actual world of being. In Plato's analogy, this cave, where the person was previously, represents the visible and perceptible world. For Plato there still existed an eternal realm of ideas. The exit from the cave, which ultimately leads to the fact that the human being is able to comprehend the world of ideas, is achieved through the development of his or her personality. Plato describes this path as an arduous process. He can only slowly free himself from the old perspectives, and outside the cave he is blinded by the bright sunlight, so he can only see things at night. Gradually, his eyes become accustomed to the brightness. But one day he is able to look into the light of the sun.

In my opinion, Plato succeeds very impressively in showing the process of human development as an arduous journey. Because one thing is certain: education and development do not drop into somebody's lap. It is never easy to give up the familiar and accustomed and embrace the new and unknown.

Whoever wants to develop his character, therefore, also needs the willingness for a process of work – or rather *cooperation* with the Holy Spirit. He wants to shape and form our personality, but we must consciously accept and allow it. Otherwise, not much will happen. One could say: Character change takes place when a person works on himself in cooperation with the Holy Spirit.

But why are we so concerned here with God's work *in* man rather than what He wants to do *through* man? I personally believe that a refined personality is more important than charisma and talent. It is not for nothing that it is said, «People are hired for their competence and fired for their character.» In the end, it is the inner attitude that counts because it is a critical factor in success – and, unfortunately, the main reason why appointed charismatic leaders fail. In most cases, they do not fail because of a lack of knowledge or competence. It is almost always due to the personality. You might come up with the following equation: Charisma minus character equals chaos. Without a character that is molded and formed by the Holy Spirit, we will not be able to be convincing in the ministry in the long run. Therefore, God wants to work *in* us first before He can work effectively *through* us.

There is no doubt that a person's character is, to a certain extent, a result of his upbringing and his innate characteristics. However, this fact should never be used as a justification for avoiding the necessary maturation processes. Being a Christian also means being open to the changes that God wants to bring about in us. He wants to transform our indifference into love, our anger into gentleness, and our lack of discipline into self-control. This intent becomes clear when Paul speaks of a life in the Spirit and lists the nine divine character traits (Gal. 5:22). The character of Christ is to become our own. In this sense, the apostle also calls us to «put on Christ» (Gal. 3:27; Rom. 13:14; Col. 3:10). It may sound a bit simplistic, but just as I choose a certain outfit every morning, I should also choose to «clothe» myself daily with the nature of Jesus Christ. Personality and character development is not a one-time thing, but a constant and conscious decision to be molded according to God's will.

Viktor Frankl expresses the value of such inner work in apt words: «Everything you have can be taken from you, but what you are, no one can take from you.» The character indicates the greatness and the richness of the inner man, which will inevitably influence his environment. In my years of ministry, I have come to realize that one's character is among the most important tools of a spiritual leader. God's method is the person himself in his character and charisma. First and foremost, he does not work with programs, concepts or talents, but with personalities. In other words: The man or woman himself is the message. Not what I say, but what I am, is accepted. Whoever wants to influence his environment and lead other people, will do this first and foremost through his character.

A person who allows his nature to be shaped by the Holy Spirit not only wins the hearts of others, but also takes care of his own heart. It is only when his thinking, his speaking, and his doing are in harmony that he can be at peace with himself. Personal integrity and authenticity are especially important for ministry because they keep us from living a double life. Lack of truthfulness, on the other hand, leads to the splitting of our personality and the destruction of our spiritual ministry.

Therefore, those who constantly work on their character do themselves the greatest favor. It is a true blessing that God has not left us alone with this task, but has given us the Holy Spirit. He wants to work on us. If we want this change, actively search for it, and allow it, God can shape and form our innermost being according to His example. This process will not always feel comfortable, because like any other school, God's school is challenging for us at times (Heb.

12:6-11). Nevertheless, it is best for us because our character will determine the success of our ministry in the long run.

❓ QUESTIONS FOR PERSONAL REFLECTION.

1. The stagnation of character development is not what God has intended. He wants us to become more and more like Jesus. How have you worked on your character development in the past?
2. Anyone who wants to develop his or her character must allow for a painful process in which the Holy Spirit is allowed to change you. What is your level of readiness in the face of the realization that there will be a price for change?

6   THE WORK OF THE HOLY SPIRIT THROUGH US

After we have looked at the meaning of grace and the necessity of the Holy Spirit's work in us, I would like to come to an essential part of this book now: God's act of grace *through* man in the power of the Holy Spirit. The word *charisma* used in this context goes back to the short word *charis*, which I explained at the beginning. *Charisma* is probably best translated as gift or gift of grace. The plural of this term – the *charismata* – is used several times in the New Testament of the Bible and refers here to the gifts or charismata / charisms of the faithful. The charis (the grace) effects the various *charismata*.

At this point I would like to briefly point out the meaning of the word "charisma" in the German language: A person with charisma is someone with a special aura; and people in leadership positions (such as politicians) have particularly good chances of being elected if they have charisma. The way the term is used here, however, has little to do with the New Testament understanding. In the NT it refers to various talents and functions in the church. These charisms are not reserved for individuals: Just as every believer has received a certain measure of grace (Eph. 4:7), according to the New Testament, he has certain gifts (1 Pet. 4:10; Rom. 12:6). Thus,

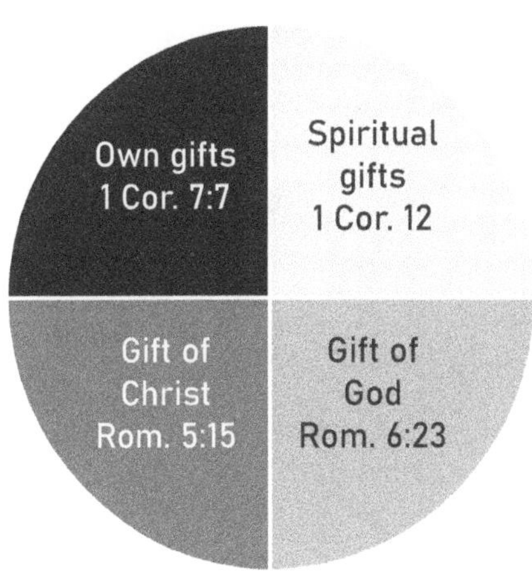

all Christians without exception are charismatic, not only a few chosen ones or a special group. Nevertheless, these charisms, similar to grace, are assigned to everyone equally, but appear in great variety.

Probably the best known list of charisms can be found in 1 Corinthians 12:8-10, where the apostle Paul introduces nine *spiritual gifts*, including the word of wisdom and the gift of faith. Other places where gifts are mentioned are in Romans 12:6-8 and 1 Peter 4:10-11 – the so-called *natural* or *personal* gifts. We are also presented with five ministries in Ephesians 4:11. These are not explicitly described as gifts, but rather as personal and office designations. Therefore, in my opinion, it seems obvious to distinguish between the *office* of the prophet and the *gift* of prophecy.

Personally, I categorize the charisms mentioned in the Bible into four categories: the gift of God, the gift of Christ, one's own gifts, and gifts of the Holy Spirit.

6.1 Gift of God and gift of Christ

The first two charisms are the gift of God and the gift of Christ (Rom. 5:15). They are the most important, because through them the Father and the Son have made salvation possible for all people. The gift of God is described in Rom. 6:23 and also in 2 Cor. 1:11 as eternal life, which the redeemed person has received from his Creator: For the wages of sin is death, but the free gift of God is eternal life in Christ Jesus our Lord. (Rom. 6:23)

Jesus' redemptive work on the cross, on the other hand, is the gift that makes eternal life possible (Rom. 5:15). Through the transgression of "the one," death was given a right to the many. Through the obedience of "the one" Jesus Christ on the cross of Calvary, a gift was given to the many, by which death lost its power over them. These two charisms are closely related and are the foundation of the others. Only those who have received them receive the others. Unfortunately, not all people accept them for their salvation.

6.2 Own gifts

Natural abilities such as singing or craftsmanship must be distinguished from the spiritual gifts. In my opinion, Paul is referring to natural gifts when he speaks of the "gift of God's grace" in 1 Corinthians 7:7, which is individually given:

I wish that all were as I myself am. But each has his own gift from God, one of one kind and one of another.

The question arises here as to why these natural abilities are called gifts of God: Why are they considered charisms, even though they are mostly shaped by the parental home, genetically inherited or acquired in one's course of life? And what does this have to do with the grace of God when a person exercises them? In my opinion, Paul wants to express that, through the new life in Christ, every little detail falls under the dominion of God. Every part of a person is accepted by the Holy Spirit and used for His service. No area of life is excluded from Christ`s reign. Therefore, it can also be said that everybody has charisms, because each one of us is gifted and everything we have can become a gift of God. Some may believe there are people who have not received any talent. I do not think that's true. Human life always means talent. No one is exempt from this blessing, but some gifts are overlooked or undervalued by our society.

In Rom. 12:6-8 we find a first overview in which Paul lists the various gifts (except for prophecy) that fall into the category of natural gifts just described.

This list does not claim to be exhaustive. Paul did not want to present an all-encompassing list of gifts, but rather to encourage the brothers and sisters in faith to develop their special abilities to the fullest potential. In Rom. 12:4ff. Paul's conviction becomes clear that each member has a specific function in the church and is urgently needed. In principle, gifts are not given to focus attention on the individual, but are given as a blessing to the community. This edification of the brothers and sisters is the primary goal of the Holy Spirit's work through us. Although the list of gifts in Rom. 12:6-8 is not complete[12], the abilities listed should not be overlooked. On the contrary, it is possible that these gifts contribute to the health and

---

12 *In the lists of the New Testament mentioned above, there are more than 20 different terms used for the gifts. The comparison with Rom. 12:6-8 suggests that Paul does not have a fixed catalog of gifts, but selects from the multitude.*

vitality of a congregation. Therefore, I will briefly outline them in the following text. In doing so the charisma mentioned first, namely prophecy, will be put aside for the time being, since it is not a natural gift. It will sufficiently be looked at in the chapter on the spiritual gifts.

SERVICE

Among the gifts now mentioned, we first encounter *diakonia*. From this Greek term the German words "Diakonie" or "Diakon" are derived. The "service", as *diakonia* can also be translated, obviously has many facets, because in 1 Cor. 12:5 Paul writes: "There are various ministries, but only one Lord." Ministry may mean, among other things, organizational or charitable tasks as described in Acts 6:1-7. The works associated with the provision of meals by which the Spirit-filled brethren relieved the apostles are described there by the same word, *diakonia*.

People with the gift of service are more capable in their particular area of action than the people they help.

They see day-to-day needs and address them. They often operate behind the scenes. Nonetheless, they do valuable work and support individual brothers and sisters or the church itself. There may be places where there are no apostles or prophets, but there are none without servants. They are invaluable to any church.

TEACHING

In the enumeration of Romans 12:6-8, diakonia is followed by the charism of teaching. Like anyone who has received a gift, the teacher is to bring his abilities to the church, writes Paul. Whether someone is suitable for teaching will be shown by his or her ministry. If he can lead learners to the knowledge of the Word of God and to grow in grace, it confirms his teaching gift. A person with this charism is not a know-it-all or a selfish person. He explains the truth and the depth of the Bible understandably and clearly. The

Holy Scriptures are not easily accessible to everyone. This is due, among other things, to the fact that the Bible did not fall from heaven, but that it was written here on earth by human authors inspired by God. Since these authors lived a long time ago in a culture that is foreign to us, people with a teaching gift can help us to overcome this gap. They build a bridge from the Bible to man and in this way provide us with access to it.

ENCOURAGEMENT

Brothers and sisters who are gifted in comforting or encouraging others are called by Paul to use this gift. At present, few churches would claim to have people with the charism of encouragement, but rather that some of their members have pastoral skills. In the end, the gift described here is probably also the pastoral skill of building people up, encouraging them, standing by them, and comforting them. Persons with this charism do not bind people to themselves, but lead them into the freedom of Christ. A biblical example of a person who probably served in the gift of encouragement is Joseph the Levite. The other apostles gave him the epithet Barnabas (which means "son of comfort"), indicating the special charism with which he encouraged others (Acts 4:36).

GIVING

All Christians should serve the work of the Lord financially by giving – only insofar they can, of course. The tithe is a good guideline that many free churches follow. If we consider all that God has given us and all that He will continue to bless us with in the future, giving should not be too challenging.

Despite this general call to give, some are gifted by God in a unique way to give their possessions to others. They are sensitive to the needs and plights of other believers and have a God-given ability to meet those needs. All this should be done in sincerity, says the text (Rom. 12:8). A person with the charism of giving is not concerned with public recognition (Mt. 6:3). He delights in giving away what God has given him to help others and to support the work of our Lord. The churches of Macedonia (2 Cor. 8:1-5) and Philippi (Phil. 4:14-18) may have had such brothers and sisters in their midst. Giving can not only help, but it can also bring a lot of joy. Where this gift is used, rejoicing is usually not long in coming!

PROTRUDING

Every organization needs wise leaders, and there is also a gift of leadership that consists of organizing and inspiring the body. A person with such a gift, like a captain on the high seas, stands at the head of his crew and gives them direction. He discerns the course set by the Holy Spirit and guides others so that they reach God's goals. Clear thinking, wisdom, and insight are among his strengths. A leader can motivate others to act and then lead them accordingly, because he has emotional intelligence. People trust his guidance and do not run away from him. In the words of John C. Maxwells: "If you think you are leading others, but no one is following you, then you are just taking a walk."[13] So it's important to fill leadership positions with talented leaders. Unfortunately, Christians often tend to place the scepter in the hands of people who have been in ministry for a long time, who are experienced members of the church, or who can devote a lot of time to a position. That alone however does not make them good leaders. A saying I hear quite often as someone is installed into a new role is, "He (or she) has been around a long time." My question in response is: "So?"

EXECUTING MERCY

Mercy is a quality of Jesus that should be attributed to all Christians. However, there are personalities who have a particularly pro-

---

13 *Maxwell: Charakter und Charisma, 13.*

nounced charism in this area. The Son of God, Jesus Christ, and His actions as a man on earth are a shining example of this. Wherever He went, the weak asked for His mercy. A person with this gift shows compassion and kindness to those who are hurting, sick, and suffering. He is willing to care for the miserable by visiting, listening, and praying. In case of an emergency, he can be reached quickly, and is always ready to listen to those in need who are sad and filled with pain. He provides practical first aid like the Good Samaritan in Jesus' parable (Lk. 10:25-37). We remember that the man who had been attacked by the robbers was also passed by people with deep theological knowledge.

However, this did not help the injured man. He would have needed the ministry of mercy.

However, the spiritual dignitaries saw no need for it. This example shows how important it is for every congregation to have brothers and sisters among the believers with this gift. Pastors are often especially thankful for them, because when the congregation reaches a certain size, it is simply no longer possible for the pastors alone to visit all those in need.

As indicated, the above list of natural gifts is by no means exhaustive. The abilities just mentioned are of particular importance for the welfare of a congregation, but there are many other talents that every local church can use. If Paul were writing this list today, there would certainly be other gifts listed that would be important for church planting today. Perhaps he would name the artists who have a sense for the aesthetic and who can produce beautiful things. We are living in the age of digitalization, and the Internet has become one of the most important tools in terms of external impact. The way the church presents itself in the media is of enormous importance for its growth. It is good to have people in our midst who can express the kingdom of God in this area as well.

Something similar can be said about the sound artists: Our era demands a certain professionalism in the field of music as well. Visitors to free churches, like the secular population, have a certain demand for music. Churches must engage with this fact. In Russian, someone once said, "There are two types of people: The ones who make music and the others, who should only listen to music." Since I, like so many others, belong to the latter group, I am very grateful for the brothers and sisters who are musically gifted.

Another gift that is not mentioned in Rom. 12:6-8, but is especially important for the Body of Jesus Christ, is hospitality. Peter demands it from the believers before he speaks about the charisms (1 Pet. 4:9) and Paul also sees it as a prerequisite for the ministry of elders (1 Tim. 3:2).

To be hospitable means to open your house to outsiders and brothers and sisters in faith. But at a time when the population of our country is increasingly fragmented into separate social milieus, we are often reluctant to let strangers into our "castle". The English saying "My home is my castle" is also true in this country. Due to the trend of urbanization, many people live side by side in a small space, and yet many of them feel lonely in the midst of people.

In Siberia a Christian woman invited my mother into her home and welcomed her into the small group that gathered under her roof. Through this open-hearted woman, my mother came to believe in Jesus Christ. A short time later my father sat in the circle of these believers. A few years later he became the pastor of our local church. We are very grateful that this woman opened her home and her heart to my mother. Just like our family, many churches are blessed by people with the gift of hospitality.

The list of valuable charisms that people bring to the community could be expanded indefinitely. But now that we have considered our own natural abilities, let's take a closer look at the specific gifts given by the Holy Spirit.

6.3 GIFTS OF THE HOLY SPIRIT

The charisms of the Spirit form the fourth group of gifts. As the attentive reader will have noticed in the previous sections, the term charism is not necessarily connected with the work of the Holy Spirit. In the case of the charisms described here, however, the action of the Spirit is explicitly given. But how can we recognize that the gifts discussed here are to be regarded as spiritual gifts?

The difference between them and the natural gifts mentioned above is that Paul not only calls them charismata in the introduction to his following treatise (1 Cor. 12:1): he also calls them pneumatika (cf. 14:1), which for the sake of simplicity I will translate simply as "effects of the Spirit":

But about the gifts of the Spirit, brothers and sisters, I will not leave you in ignorance.

Shortly thereafter, Paul also refers to the same phenomenon as "manifestations of the Spirit" (1 Cor. 12:7). All of these terms stand for the same gifts or effects that emanate from the Spirit, and they are now mentioned in his following remarks.

There are diversities of gifts, but the same Spirit. There are differences of ministries, but the same Lord. And there are diversities of activities, but it is the same God who works all in all. (1 Cor. 12:4-6)

The various charisms are given to born-again Christians by the Holy Spirit for the buildup of the church (1 Cor. 12:7). In other words, the Holy Spirit endows people with charisms in order to strengthen those around them. This connection is also shown in the further course of the first letter to the Corinthians (chap. 12-14), where the gifts of the Spirit are associated in several passages with benefit or edification. Their sphere of influence is foremost in the assembly of the church. This is especially evident in 1 Cor. 14. The Holy Spirit does not distribute the gifts so that an individual can stand out, shine, or distinguish himself. Nor are they given to the believer to build himself up. Instead the gifts of the Spirit are to be a blessing to others - that is and remains their purpose. If they do not serve this purpose, they become meaningless. Only the gift of tongues can be practiced for one's own good, as we will see later. For the rest, however, the following applies: Let all things be done for the edification of the church (1 Cor. 14:12, 26). It is not for nothing that Peter speaks of the so-called "gifts of ministry" in this context (1 Pet. 4:10).

The fact that Paul writes[14] about the gifts of the Spirit with great matter-of-factness is, in my opinion, clear evidence of a vibrant spiritual culture in the early church. Obviously, things were much more charismatic than in our churches today. Paul does not even attempt to write a systematic doctrine of the works of the Holy Spirit; he speaks of spiritual gifts only to deal with grievances in the individual churches. If he had done this, the number of testimonies for the works of the Holy Spirit among the first Christians would probably be much larger.

ALLOCATION OF GIFTS AND THEIR HANDLING

Charisms cannot be learned or bought. We can simply receive them, like grace. The first letter to the Corinthians says that the Holy Spirit gives them "as he wills" (1 Cor. 12:11). Although charisms are gifts that are given, Christians are urged to strive for them at the same time (1 Cor. 12:31; 14:1). God wants to collaborate with people in this area as well. They should longingly desire to be used by the Holy Spirit and to cooperate with Him. Unfortunately, my experience shows me that this is not always the case. Is it possible that churches today are losing their spiritual power because Christians are no longer seeking spiritual gifts? Disinterest and passivity will not get us there. In my opinion, we should be constantly seeking to be used by the Spirit of God for the edification of His church. Why else would Paul so obviously advise us to do so?

Some Christians may be skeptical about spiritual gifts – perhaps because they have seen their misuse or abuse. But such unpleasant experiences should not lead to a complete abandonment of the

---

14 *We find mentions not only in the First Corinthians, but also in Gal. 3:5; 1 Thess. 5:19-22; 1 Tim. 4:14.*

  The work of the Holy Spirit through us

charisms. On the contrary, we are challenged to learn from our mistakes and get it right in the future. When the Holy Spirit works through people, God and man cooperate closely to produce good things together. This cooperation is a great gift to man, but it is also a great challenge. We must learn to cope with the tensions that arise from it.

If we handle the gifts correctly, there is a "wonderful" interaction between God and man. Spiritual gifts in particular have the potential to edify, encourage, and correct not only individuals but entire communities. But I have also seen that an improper use of the charisms can lead to astonishment and skepticism.

We must not see the human being as a channel that receives God's words on the one hand and then passes them on unfiltered on the other hand. Rather, each believer is a messenger who always transmits the divine word and work according to his or her own personality, nature, and character (2 Cor. 5:20; Eph. 6:20). Even when the Scriptures were first written, God did not eliminate the peculiarities of the individual writers, but rather used their character, as the example of Luke shows (Lk. 1:1-4). Therefore, character should always precede charisma.

As far as prophecy is concerned, it was already obvious in New Testament times that a careful examination is needed. This is also (or especially) true when someone claims to speak on behalf of God. In his letter to the Corinthians, Paul gives clear instructions on how to avoid error and harm. Among other things, the church is to judge the impressions of prophets:

Let two or three prophets speak, and let the others weigh what is said. (1 Cor. 14:29)

It is clear that the apostle is concerned with the reflection of prophetic words by the congregation. Paul first speaks about the evaluation of prophecy in the well-known verse from 1 Thessalonians that is often quoted for all kinds of evaluations:

Do not despise prophecies, but test everything; hold fast what is good. (1 Thess. 5:20f.)

What is true of prophetic impressions is also true of the other spiritual gifts: Whenever charisms come to work through people, they should be spiritually evaluated. In this way, we can hold on to and apply the good that comes from God.

Since every gift is given through human beings and requires this test, no one who serves in the charisms should present his or her speech as the absolute word of God. It is therefore also advisable to avoid the popular phrase "Thus says the Lord...".[15] Of course, it is not about the right formula. One person may say, "The Spirit of God revealed to me..."; another, "The Word of God spoke to me...". The next one says, "I received the spiritual impression...". It does not matter how the individual chooses to express it in each particular case. What is important, however, is that he does not pass off his ministry in the respective spiritual gift as a perfect work of God and thus makes himself untouchable. The human being remains an imperfect being and cannot claim to be flawless. Those who are not willing to be tested are not qualified to serve in the spiritual gifts.

The evaluation of spiritual gifts should be twofold: content and effect. First, it must be determined whether the content of the message is divine in nature - and in this regard the Bible is the sole guide to what is said (Acts 17:11). Secondly it is necessary to assess whether the charismatic ministry also has a positive effect, because God always uses his gifts in a goal-oriented way. A charism only fulfills its purpose if it proves to be a blessing for people. If this is not the case, or if it becomes clear that its use is pointless or even harmful to other people, then it is in dire need of a closer look.

---

15 *This messenger formula was typical of the Old Testament prophets. In the New Testament, we find such a formula of authority only rudimentarily in the prophet Agabus (Acts 21:11) or in the extraordinary Revelation of John. The words of the Old Testament prophets were direct words from God, and therefore were not to be tested. This formula can be taken authoritatively, leaving the hearer little choice. It is not the nature of New Testament prophecy to be tested.*

   The work of the Holy Spirit through us

It becomes clear that ministry in the gifts always involves responsibility – whether they are working through us at the moment, whether we are receiving them, or whether we are testing them. I would like to encourage the congregation to have a wide heart, to be willing to learn, and to allow correction. No one has all wisdom and knowledge (1 Cor. 13:9f.). No one has all the gifts. Just as the development of our personality is never complete, we remain learners in our charismatic ministry. The Holy Spirit wants to work through us; and we are called to give him room and to grow in our gifts.

THE THREE CATEGORIES OF SPIRITUAL GIFTS

It seems to me that the spiritual gifts listed in 1 Corinthians 12 can very well be divided into categories. As mentioned above, Paul probably did not work systematically, but rather responded to the challenges the Corinthians were facing. In general, God wants to communicate His grace in many different ways, and the Holy Spirit cannot be forced into our concepts. Therefore, my classification is not to be understood as dogma, but merely an attempt to present the gifts from 1 Cor. 12:8-9 in a clear way. I am going to divide them into three categories for a better overview: The gifts of revelation, the gifts of power, and the gifts of tongues.

The gifts of power demonstrate God's strength and greatness in a visible way. God's grace shows itself visually. The gifts of revelation, on the other hand, bring out what is hidden. They give insight into special thoughts and intentions of God. The gifts of tongues communicate God's intentions audibly. They can therefore also be called auditory gifts.

These three categories show that God uses different ways of communicating His grace to people. We human beings are no different: we love to interact – in many ways. It is not without reason that the professional field of media communication has grown rapidly. One of our basic needs is to communicate, and I am convinced that God Himself has endowed us with the will and the ability to communi-

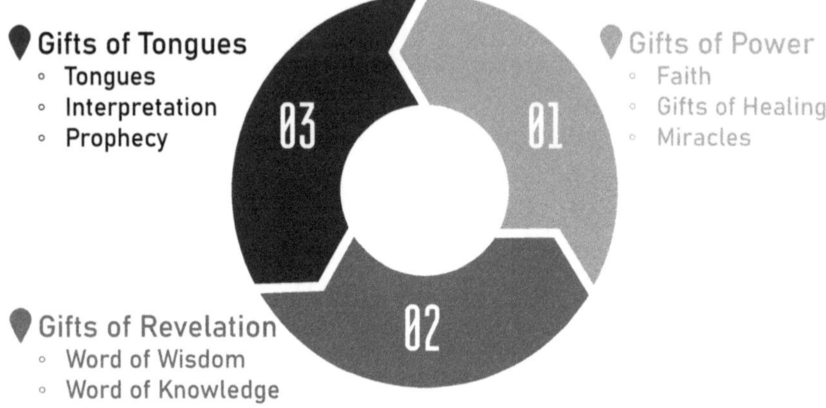

cate. The spiritual gifts can serve us as a means of communicating God's grace.

Generally, I believe that no one unites all spiritual gifts, although the Holy Spirit can activate several gifts in one person simultaneously. Normally, several people work together with their spiritual gifts like the fingers of one hand: Each one of them is important and performs certain functions, but only together do they enable the hand to perform its service. When we were created, God certainly did not have lone warriors in mind, but rather team players - people who depend on each other and need each other's support. For this reason, anyone who wants to serve in the spiritual gifts should have a high degree of humility and modesty. Those who allow their nature to be shaped in this way have the best prerequisites for receiving the gifts, for God gives His grace only to the humble (Prov. 3:34; Mt. 23:12; Jas. 4:6; 1 Pet. 5:5).

The colorful bouquet of spiritual gifts that God gives us fascinates me. It corresponds to the diversity of human beings and their way of communicating in different ways. In the following chapters, I will take a closer look at each of the spiritual gifts and share some of my practical experiences with them.

Despite the matter-of-factness with which the effects of the Spirit were apparently manifested in the early Christian congregations, these phenomena diminished as church history progressed. Only isolated groups still sought to receive and walk in the gifts of the Holy Spirit. In this context, reference is often made to Paul, who in the famous 13th chapter of first Corinthians speaks of prophecy and tongues ceasing one day (1 Cor. 13:8). But the question arises whether that day has already come. "Yes!" say some. They say that they, like the other effects of the Spirit, are limited to the apostolic age and have not been needed since the writing of the New Testament texts. The fact that the spiritual gifts seem to have disappeared more and more in the course of the subsequent church history seems to confirm this way of understanding the text.

A large part of Christianity, however, interprets the texts of the New Testament differently – and in my opinion rightly so. Paul does indeed mention a time limit for this form of the work of the Holy Spirit, but he is not talking about the present, but of the eschatological future. The context of the text also points to the correctness of this interpretation: We can conclude that the Corinthians believed that they had already reached the goal, so they did not even assume a resurrection of the dead (1 Cor. 15:12). From their point of view, the work of the Spirit was a confirmation of their completion (1 Cor. 14:20ff.). But Paul enlightened them and made it clear that the work of the Holy Spirit would also cease when the kingdom of God came in its fullness. The gifts of the Spirit would then no longer be necessary (1 Cor. 13:8ff.). For this reason, knowledge will also pass away, but love will endure forever (1 Cor. 13:13). Therefore, everyone should strive for it, but for the time being also for the other gifts (14:1). The apostle's real concern was obviously to make it clear to the Corinthians that a time would come when gifts would no longer be needed. However, the fact that they were still being manifested at this time should give the Corinthians pause.

Through the Gospels we also know about the more detailed spiritual contexts that still exist in our time: The kingdom of God has already "come near" with Jesus Christ (Mk. 1:15) and the work of the Holy Spirit confirms this (Mk. 9:1). However, it also remains in the future and is still pending (Mk. 10:23; Lk. 14:15 etc.). Therefore, we still ask in the Lord's Prayer, the prayer that our Lord taught us, for his kingdom to come. It has already begun, but it is not yet completed. Given the context described above, I believe it is impossible to sustain the hypothesis that Paul intended to imply that the workings of the Holy Spirit were limited to the apostolic age.

Whoever takes Paul seriously and reads the Scriptures carefully can really only come to the conclusion that these gifts are available to us until our perfection at Jesus' return.

Nevertheless, such manifestations are rare in our churches. Why is it that Christians are so reserved about these effects of the Holy Spirit? It is likely that one of the decisive factors for this close-mindedness lies in the Western view of the world, to which such phenomena are simply foreign. Moreover, it is well known that gifts can be the cause of misuse or unintentional harm. As in other areas of life, the best way to avoid such misfortunes is to find and eliminate the cause. I have already emphasized that it is better to learn from mistakes than to avoid the work of the Spirit. Therefore, we are challenged to examine and develop our spiritual gifts.

This process of evaluation always reminds me of the work of the gold diggers. Whoever wanted to find a treasure had to remove a lot of soil and dirt to get to the precious goods. It is similar with the gifts. Not everything that comes to light in seeking the charisms is gold, and in human words we also encounter much that is human. Even as God's instruments we remain fallible creatures. It is up to us to bring out the gold in what is being said. In my opinion, this is the real concern of the apostle Paul, when he calls on the church to "keep" and apply the good that is passed on through the gifts (1 Thess. 5:20f.).

Our Lord Jesus Christ has given His Church precious gifts that were of great importance in early Christianity. It would be unfortunate if, given our worldview or fear of mistakes and misfortunes, we would forego these charisms. I personally choose to make room for the work of the Holy Spirit in my life!

❓ QUESTIONS FOR PERSONAL REFLECTION.

1.   According to the New Testament no human being is ungifted. Every believer has received some measure of grace, and everyone is also gifted. Are you aware of your gifts?
2.   If you did not answer «yes» to the previous question, what are some ways to get to know your gifts?
3.   How do you feel about the effects of the Holy Spirit? From your point of view, are they desirable, or are they rather alien to you?

7 THE BAPTISM OF THE SPIRIT

Before going into the details of the gifts of the Spirit, it is necessary to speak of a peculiarity that is important in the context of the charisms. It is not understood as a condition for receiving the gifts, since the prerequisite is rebirth. It is nonetheless important for the development of the charisms of the Holy Spirit. After being born again, there is another special experience that is recorded in the Bible: The baptism in the Holy Spirit, which was poured out on Pentecost. Every year, believers around the world celebrate the Feast of Pentecost. In particular, people who share a personal experience of Pentecost with the early Christians use the feast as an opportunity to celebrate the distinctive features of their faith – including the baptism in the Spirit. Some Christians know about Pentecost but believe they have little to gain from the baptism in the Spirit: They have already been baptized and received the Holy Spirit. Why would it be necessary for them to undergo a second, mysterious baptism? But one question is justified: What is the baptism in the Spirit really about? The Bible does not actually know the term baptism in the spirit. The New Testament speaks about "baptism with the Holy Spirit". Shortly before his ascension, Jesus spoke to his disciples about the promise of the Father. He advised them to wait in Jerusalem and then told them:

John baptized with water, but you shall be baptized with the Holy Spirit. (Acts 1:5)

What Jesus had already pointed out before was finally to come true. It is reported in all the gospels (Mt. 3:11; Mk. 1:8; Lk. 3:16; Jn. 1:32f.). The disciples to whom Jesus now spoke had followed him for three years. They had come to know him intensively, had heard his teachings, believed in him, and received assurance of salvation and authority.
But they still lacked one crucial experience – the power of the Holy Spirit that would enable them to be witnesses for Jesus (Acts 1:8).

The disciples had already been baptized. In addition, they had already received the Holy Spirit from the risen Lord on Easter Eve (Jn. 20:20). Nevertheless, there was something they were asked to wait for (Lk. 24:49). It was not yet time to leave Jerusalem and carry out the Great Commission. Instead, they were given a second experience with the Spirit of God, which they still needed. This prediction was fulfilled on the day of Pentecost when the Holy Spirit fell upon the waiting disciples (Acts 2:2-4). As promised, they spoke in other languages and received power. Their subsequent ministry was accompanied by the supernatural work of the Holy Spirit.

Peter interpreted this event as the fulfillment of the prophecies of Joel (Joel 3:1-4; Acts 2:15-20). Through him, God had promised that in the last days He would pour out His Spirit in a special way on all His followers. Through this spirit they would receive dreams and prophecies, among other things. Not everything that Joel had predicted came to pass at that time, but the time which Joel had spoken of began on that day. It is also noticeable in this context that Peter did not speak of the fact that the prophecy of Joel had been completely fulfilled, but merely that this miraculous event was "spoken of" by the prophet (Acts 2:16).

We are more likely to find closer connections to the baptism in the Holy Spirit in the gospel of Luke. Paul, on the other hand, contributed little to the doctrine of the baptism in the Spirit. Although he does not explicitly mention it, his statement in 1 Cor. 12:3 is an indication of its existence. Nevertheless, this verse is difficult to use as a reference to the baptism in the Spirit. But in chapters 12-14 of First Corinthians, Paul makes an equally clear connection as Luke (Lk. 24:49) between receiving the Spirit and receiving His power.

In terms of salvation and history, Pentecost was a one-time event. The time of the Holy Spirit has thus begun. From now on, God wants to be present among people through the working of His Spirit. The Spirit is to inspire preaching (1 Cor. 2:1-16; Eph. 1:17), convict of sin, righteousness and judgment (Jn. 16:8), produce faith (2 Cor. 4:13; Gal. 5:5), dwell in the believer (Rom. 8:9), give salvation, sonship to God, and assurance of salvation (Jn. 3:5; Rom. 8:4-16; Tit. 3:5), and distribute gifts for the edification of the church (1 Cor. 12-14). Many more could be mentioned, but all these effects do not describe the baptism in the Spirit, for this refers to the experience of the disciples at Pentecost. And this experience, according to Peter, is a promise of the Father to all the children of God – even today: The Pentecost event was unique, but the Pentecost experience is repeatable and everyone can have his own personal Pentecost, if he only sincerely asks for it (Acts 2:39; 4:31).

I once had a conversation with an acquaintance of mine about this promise of the baptism in the Spirit while we were out for a walk. I tried to explain that today, more than ever, we depend on His power to be witnesses. But my acquaintance initially waved it off: "What do I need that for? I am already a child of God." I replied that this was also about a precious promise of the Father. He was puzzled, thought about it, and then said: "Okay, I want to receive it. Right now!" We were walking through the broadly laid out cemetery in our neighborhood. I looked around for a moment and said to him, "Let's go home. I'll be happy to pray for you there." But he sank to his knees - ready to receive God's gift. What else could I do? I blessed him and he experienced the baptism of the Holy Spirit.

The baptism in the Spirit is not an end in itself. Nor is it awarded like a trophy for mere possession. As always when God gives something, there is a clear purpose. Here too: The proclamation of the Gospel is to be done in power. As Christians, our calling is to be witnesses for our Lord - that is our Great Commission.

However, we are not to do this out of our own ability, but in the power of His strength, drawing from God's possibilities. The baptism in the Spirit opens the door for us to this power of the Spirit. It makes us strong and courageous so that we can be firm witnesses for Jesus. Jesus' disciples already experienced this crucial difference: After the crucifixion they had locked themselves away "for fear of the Jews" (Jn. 20:19). Great had been their grief and fear. But after the Risen Lord had baptized them with the Holy Spirit, they were courageous and determined. Even prison could not stop them from continuing to speak about Jesus (Acts 5:17-21). Through the baptism in the Holy Spirit, they had become completely different personalities.

This strength or power wrought by the Holy Spirit is necessary to persevere in the spiritual ministry and preach the Gospel. Some may be very well educated or have special knowledge, but if the spiritual power is lacking, one is not in a good position.

We rightly state that *being born again to new life* is the fundamental work of the Holy Spirit. But the logical next step is baptism in the Holy Spirit. If we are to take the book of Acts seriously, we must distinguish between these two events: First they came to believe in Jesus Christ, then they were baptized with the Holy Spirit. This order can be seen in the events in Samaria and Ephesus (Acts 8:12-17; 19:1-7). Baptism in the Holy Spirit is not to be equated with regeneration. Nor is it to be regarded as a special form of sanctification. The baptism in the Holy Spirit does not elevate a Christian to a special spiritual state so that one can be proud of it. It cannot be earned, nor can it be called a special distinction for anything. No one can boast about being baptized in the Holy Spirit.

I must clearly contradict the assumption that this experience is foremost for spiritual leaders or experienced Christians.

The baptism in the Holy Spirit is open to all believers of all backgrounds. Personally, I think it is best for people to experience the baptism of the Spirit immediately after conversion and the baptism of faith, as Peter promised his listeners after his Pentecost sermon (Acts 2:38). The biblical accounts do not indicate any specific way in which the baptism in the Spirit should have manifested itself. Only one thing was clear: Its effects were unmistakable. Being baptized in the Spirit has always been accompanied by visible signs – usually by speaking in tongues (Acts 2:4; 10:46; 19:6), but also by power (4:31), prophecy (19:6), or praise (2:11; 10:46). How exactly people experience the baptism in the Spirit today is left to God. In any case, it is important not to exert pressure.

The question remains whether there are other prerequisites besides regeneration for Christians to receive the baptism of the Holy Spirit. Yes, I would say that expectation and faith play an important role.

Only the thirsty will drink and only the one who believes will receive. What a person should bring is the willingness to serve and to fulfill the Great Commission, for the baptism in the Spirit is the equipment of power for this purpose and should be used as such.

The baptism in the Spirit is given to the believer in prayer, and Jesus Christ Himself is the baptizer. However, it is still recommended not to ask for this alone. The disciples were gathered as a community when the Holy Spirit came upon them at Pentecost. If a Christian asks together with the brothers and sisters for the baptism in the Spirit, he will be strengthened and encouraged in his faith by the others. In addition, our Lord promises us that he wants to be present among us when we are gathered together in twos or threes (Mt. 18:20).

Some of us may not feel edified by certain people in our spiritual environment. I would like to urge these brothers and sisters not to let everyone of them be their advisor in this area. I come from a rather evangelical-baptist background, and there the baptism in the Holy Spirit was viewed very critically. When I started to reach out for the baptism in the Holy Spirit, I was warned by some of the Christians in my environment.

One even told me, "You better watch out! You could receive an evil spirit." But I decided to trust in the wonderful promise of Jesus:

If then you who are evil know how to give good gifts to your children, how much more will the Father in heaven give the Holy Spirit to those who ask him. (Lk. 11:13)

The same will happen to those who earnestly ask for the baptism in the Holy Spirit. Christians often allow themselves to be deprived of the blessings of the Spirit - the reasons are unbelief, doubt, fear of man, anxiety, indifference, disinterest, and many more. But whoever wants to receive it should desire it and look forward to it, just as a child looks forward to unwrapping his birthday present. One thing is certain: The baptism in the Spirit will challenge our faith. It makes us dependent on our Creator and on the work of His Spirit. But we can understand it as a wonderful gift from God. We need His power equipment for witnessing because He wants all people to be saved (Acts 2:38; 1 Tim. 2:4).

It should be mentioned at this point that in addition to the one-time baptism, the Bible also speaks of being filled with the Holy Spirit on a regular basis (Eph. 5:18). However, we are not talking about intoxication with the Spirit, as this passage is sometimes misunderstood. The juxtaposition of wine and spirit might lead some people to such an interpretation. But nothing of the sort is said: The Ephesians were not to get drunk on wine, as was the custom in their environment during religious ceremonies, but to be filled with the Holy Spirit. Paul was certainly thinking of a worship service or other gatherings and situations in which the Holy Spirit comes upon believers and works among them. When we let our innermost being be filled with the Holy Spirit, other useless things are flushed out and God's Spirit can expand in us, shape us, and guide us.

Living a life in the abundance of the power of the Holy Spirit will make us strong for our daily challenges and bring us into a deeper understanding of God's Word and the person of Jesus (Jn. 16:8-11, 14). Thus, after the ascension of Jesus, the baptism with the Spirit of God became an important part of the Christian life.

The following charts are intended to help the reader better understand this second experience of the Holy Spirit at Pentecost. They serve only as a structural aid and do not claim to be complete. The spiritual realities mentioned here are not to be understood as static as they appear at first glance, for spiritual life is also in a constant state of flux.

TEXT	LOCA-TION	DESIGNA-TION	SIGNS
Acts 2:4	Jerusalem	Filled with the Spirit	Visible signs, Speaking in tongues
Acts 8:17f.	Samaria	Receiving the Spirit	Visible signs
Acts 9:17	Damascus	Filling of the Holy Spirit	Healing
Acts 10:45f.	Caesarea	Outpouring of the Spirit	Speaking in tongues
Acts 19:6	Ephesus	Coming of the Spirit	Speaking in tongues, Prophecy

EASTER	PENTECOST
Rebirth	Baptism in the Spirit
Christ in man	Christ through man
Work of the Holy Spirit in man	Work of the Holy Spirit through man
Character of Jesus	Ministry of Jesus
Fruit of the Spirit	Unfolding of the fruit
Gifts of the Spirit	Unfolding of the gifts

? QUESTIONS FOR PERSONAL REFLECTION.

1.   Although the baptism in the Spirit is well attested in the Bible, it is not known to all believers. Has this chapter changed your view on this subject?

2.   The baptism in the Spirit is a gift from our Lord to His witnesses, and for the apostles it was a necessity. Nevertheless, many Christians are indifferent to it. Do you want to open yourself to this second experience with the Holy Spirit?

8 GIFTS OF REVELATION

8.1 THE WORD OF WISDOM

Let us now turn to the gifts of the Spirit in detail, as we classified them in chapter 6 for a better overview. Paul begins the enumeration of the nine gifts of the Spirit in 1 Corinthians 12 with the "word of wisdom":

To one is given by the Spirit the word of wisdom ... (1 Cor. 12:8)

Together with the "word of knowledge" and the "gift of the discernment of spirits", we count the "word of wisdom" as one of the three gifts of revelation. What is to be understood by this "speech of wisdom"? Let us take another look at the Bible. Paul explains at the beginning of his letter, that a distinction must be made between divine and worldly wisdom: Measured by worldly standards, the preached Gospel – the "word of the cross" – is foolishness (1 Cor. 1:19-27). The wisdom of God must therefore be accessed spiritually. Paul emphasizes that his teaching is not based on human wisdom, but also on supernatural wisdom (1 Cor. 2:6, 7, 13).

The Greek word used here for wisdom is "*sophia*". It refers to the ability to behave correctly in a wide variety of situations in life. One could also say: wisdom is applied knowledge. Knowledge without doing the right thing, on the other hand, is folly. At this point, some Bible translations speak of the "gift of passing on wisdom". Unfortunately, this translation is misleading, because it does not say "*gift* of wisdom" here, but "*word* of wisdom". The exact wording is critical, because it refers to a significant detail: It indicates that this work of the Spirit is not always available, but is selective. This distinction is important because it does not mean that a person has the fullness of God's wisdom.

It is only received once in a while. The assumption that it has to do with particular education or special knowledge is also misleading. The word of wisdom is given by the Holy Spirit after all (1 Cor. 12:7).

So it is not about the person and his wisdom, but about the Holy Spirit, who wants to work according to His sovereign will. Therefore, the word of wisdom is not a product of our mind or intellect, but a gift of God. Whoever exercises it always remains under the guidance and instruction of the Most High.

A person can have human intelligence, knowledge, and wisdom and still not have spiritual wisdom. Overwhelming questions will always arise. In spite of all his education and wisdom, in many cases he remains helpless. Therefore, it is a blessing to have a source of wisdom that is supernatural.

For the Lord gives wisdom; from his mouth come knowledge and understanding. (Prov. 2:6)

In this context, I remember a difficult conversation. I had a few years ago.

A person who is very dear to me sought my advice. As I listened to her, countless wise thoughts poured into my head. But I felt that it did not come down to my education or the books I had read, but the wisdom of God. After the conversation, I called a friend and asked him to give me his impressions about it. He confronted me with a razor-sharp word of wisdom. It was immediately clear to me what I needed to do. Such spiritually effective moments of wisdom are something I would not want to miss.

But how does the word of wisdom manifest itself, and in what situations is it needed? I notice that the question of How often arouses more curiosity than the question of *What* or *What for*; perhaps because the Bible does not say much about the How either. The Bible reports a number of incidents in which God's wisdom is applied to a concrete situation: It is written, for example, that the deacon Stephen spoke in the Spirit and in wisdom in a dispute with some of his critics (Acts 6:8-10).

He was able to do this because he was under the guidance of the Holy Spirit. Unfortunately, we do not learn exactly how the Holy Spirit guided and inspired him. Perhaps He put the words directly into his mouth or gave him thoughts. Or He may have given Stephen an inner certainty of the heart, which he then expressed in his own way. Jesus also often answered with inimitable wisdom - for example, on the question of paying taxes to the emperor (Lk. 20:24f.). Similarly, in this situation the exact path of inspiration remains unknown to us. I think that a word of wisdom can manifest itself in manifold forms, because the Holy Spirit also comes to us in many different ways. For example, He can remind us of the Word of God (Jn. 14:26; Ps. 119:105) or take us inside (Acts 4:8); but He can also guide our thinking and speaking (Rom. 8:14; Gal. 5:18) or give us visions, dreams, images, and impressions (Acts 2:16-18). The Spirit of God has unlimited possibilities when it comes to reaching us. One thing is certain: He makes Himself felt, and when His work is manifested, it will be different from all that is intrinsic, human and habitual. What is important is that we recognize how much we need the wisdom of God – for church life as well as for our personal daily lives. When challenges arise that are difficult to overcome, the Holy Spirit inspires us so that answers emerge that cannot be found by human means. Words of wisdom are needed to edify and nurture the church. They protect from division, smooth the waters, lead to right decisions, and reveal wrong ways – to only name a few of the numerous blessings. In addition, God's wisdom teaches us right behavior and a way of life that pleases God; it helps us in moments of important decisions and trains our discernment (1 Cor. 6:5; Eph. 5: 15; Col. 1:9; 4:5; Jas. 3:13).

We need the impulses of the Holy Spirit, otherwise we will only live from our own limited experience. We are dependent on learning - and sometimes to change our thinking completely.

In the Old Testament Proverbs, the core of biblical wisdom literature, true wisdom is closely related to closeness to God. When people live in a God-fearing way, it begins to blossom (Prov. 9:10). It leads us to insight, understanding, prudence, decisiveness, and readiness for correction (e.g. Prov. 1:5; 3:7; 4:5; 8:12; 10:8). Those who are shaped by God's wisdom will be peaceful, kind, yielding, merciful, and sincere (Jas. 3:17-18). Therefore, we should desire it and let it nourish our innermost being. If we eat food that is not good for us, it can take us days to process this bad decision. It is the same with spiritual nourishment: We should be careful to saturate ourselves with God's wisdom. Because if we do so, it will enrich and inspire our lives (Rom. 8:11-14). As a gift of the Spirit that only comes into effect selectively, the word of wisdom may seem less significant. However, the opposite is the case: especially believers who carry responsibility need it often. I remember many meetings in which we, as elders of the congregation, could not see the right way. In those hours, a word of wisdom at the right time was a tremendous relief. We finally knew what to do and the helplessness was gone. What's more, I have often been at the end of my rope in dealing with the people around me. After I had applied all the advice from the relevant literature and every single one of them proved to be fruitless, we asked the Lord for wisdom, as we are told in the letter of James (1:5). When it was clear to us how we were supposed to act, we would often ask ourselves, "Why didn't we think of asking God about this sooner?"

Therefore, I encourage every believer, like Paul and James did, to seek the gift of the word of wisdom but also ask for divine wisdom altogether (1 Cor. 12:31; 14:1; Jas. 1:5).

8.2 THE WORD OF KNOWLEDGE

Wisdom and knowledge in the biblical language are like two shoes that belong together It is no coincidence that Paul lists the word of knowledge immediately after the word of wisdom in his list of spiritual gifts.

For to one is given through the Spirit the utterance of wisdom, and to another the utterance of knowledge according to the same Spirit... (1 Cor. 12:8)

Nor is there any talk here of the "*gift* of knowledge," as if a person were to have a permanent and all-encompassing insight into all things. Furthermore, it is not about a gift of passing on knowledge, such as those with a teaching gift. We are talking about the "*word* of knowledge". The selective occurrence of the spiritual gifts becomes clear again: In a certain situation, a person receives a word from heaven through spiritual inspiration. This is a minimal fraction, but not the fullness of God-given knowledge – just as a single pearl does not form a whole pearl necklace, but only a small part of it. Knowledge is always a patchwork (1 Cor. 13:9). This insight teaches us humility toward ourselves and understanding toward others.

The word of *wisdom* is said in Scripture to be given "by the Spirit" (*dia tou pneumatos*); the word of *knowledge* is said to be given "by the same Spirit" (*kata to auto pneuma*). This difference is small, but not insignificant: the word of knowledge is given according to the norm or in accordance with the nature of the Holy Spirit. Therefore, a word of knowledge will always confirm and bring to the fore the Holy Scriptures inspired by the Spirit of God (2 Tim. 3:16; 2 Pet. 1:21). In addition, the way Paul uses the word knowledge (e.g., in Rom. 15:14; 1 Cor. 1:5) suggests that the word of knowledge gives a deeper insight into the meaning of individual passages of Scripture. It updates the Word of God, shows connections, and makes us aware of its contents. While the word of wisdom offers a practical way out of a difficult question or situation, the word of knowledge reveals biblical correlations that are important connections in the present.

When essential insights have been lost in church history, there have always been times when God has revealed His truth through people. The most famous example is probably the reformer Martin Luther; others include John Wesley and Methodism, the Baptists and Pentecostals, to name just a few individuals and renewal movements.

I remember a situation where we, as leaders of the congregation, wanted to make a decision that we thought was reasonable. But then we were pointed to a passage of Scripture in the New Testament and its meaning, which we had not been aware of until that point. Based on the Scriptures, we reconsidered our decision and were saved from making a wrong decision. I would like to emphasize once again that the word of knowledge is not intellectual knowledge that someone has acquired through diligence and study. It is rather about spirit-given insights. The Holy Spirit acts as both initiator and revealer at the same time, just as in the famous biblical example, when Jesus responded to Peter's confession of Christ:

...Flesh and blood have not revealed this to you, but my Father who is in heaven. (Mt. 16:17)

So the insight of the disciple described here was not a human insight either, but Peter was passing on a revelation from God. We also need such spiritually inspired insights in our congregational and personal lives – especially when we tend to rely a lot on our intellect. On the other hand, words of knowledge must never replace thorough Bible study.

On the contrary, our discipline and passion for immersing ourselves in the Word of God should increase. We need both, because if the Holy Spirit is the great "Reminder" of the Word of God (Jn. 14:26), then there must also be something in our hearts that He can remind us of. Therefore, it is important not to pit the word of knowledge against Bible study: Not "either or" but "both and"!

Knowledge and wisdom must go together like the left shoe goes with the right. Together they form the footwear that we need for the road ahead. Mere knowledge is of little use if it does not lead to application. At various points in my pastorate, the Holy Spirit revealed to me that I was no longer being led by my calling, but by the needs I saw. On the other hand, I was not (and never will be) able to meet all the needs. So several times in my life I have been faced with the challenge of making something of this realization. In order to see through the situation, I needed insight, but in order to change it, I needed wisdom. There is hardly a person who has never been in such a predicament. Everyone gets into a situation where he loses sight of the big picture. Then he needs not only God's wisdom, but also knowledge. What a blessing it is that the Holy Spirit who dwells in us wants to bring both.

Knowledge is also insight. If I enter a dark room, I will not be able to perceive anything at first. But as soon as I turn on the light, I have insight into the actual conditions of the room: I can see what is in front of me and where I can go. Knowledge is gained in the place where God brings light into our dark situations. Thus, knowledge has to do with insight, understanding, and discernment.

Some time ago, I got into a conversation with a person who was very confused. He had a feeling that he was in a state of disorientation. He had many dreams at night and couldn't shake the feeling that God wanted to speak to him. But what did these dreams mean? He would have preferred to hear my interpretations. But it is much better to ask the Lord for knowledge and insight. He gives them gladly. I have often experienced that God has spoken through dreams or supernatural intuitions, and then He has given the necessary insight so that His words could be properly understood. And yet, not all dreams are from the Lord, either. I pointed this out to the person and advised him to ask God for knowledge - and for patience. For if there is no clarity at first, we can practice long-suffering. Not everything is immediately clear to us. The famous philosopher Sören Kierkegaard put it well: "We live forward, but often understand backward."

Dealing with knowledge is always a challenge. There are two dangers that spiritual leaders face in particular. The first is that knowledge is lost. In Hosea 4:6 God addresses the priesthood and says:

My people are destroyed for lack of knowledge; because you have rejected knowledge, I reject you from being a priest to me.

These are harsh words. In ancient Israel, the priests were among the spiritual leaders. They were jointly responsible for the spiritual well-being of the people. But when they disregarded God and his word, they lost the necessary knowledge for their ministry. Jesus also spoke of the scribes and Pharisees who wanted to follow their own insights rather than God's: "They are blind guides for the blind." (Mt.15:14) This makes it clear that the knowledge of God's Word is especially important for leaders and should always be desired and sought after.

The second danger in dealing with knowledge is exactly the opposite – namely, that we think we have gained a particularly large amount of insight: we read in 1 Cor. 8:1 that knowledge can puff us up. When the first Christian congregations were formed, there were many false teachers with strange insights. Many of these special teachings were summarized under the Greek collective term "gnosis" (knowledge). Even then, Paul warned against such Gnostics who caused confusion with their secret special knowledge:

Avoid the irreverent babble and contradictions of what is falsely called "knowledge". (1 Tim. 6:20)

The words the apostle used here are rather sharp. But they were meant to protect his disciple Timothy from getting into useless discussions with such people. These words can also admonish us and prevent us from coming up with special teachings and becoming arrogant. Knowledge is essentially something very positive. However, as always, the right handling of things is important. Even the best food can kill a person. Therefore, Christ must be in our focus so that the gifts can be a blessing to us and to others. Colossians 2:3 says that in Him "all the treasures of wisdom and knowledge are hidden." True knowledge is found when we seek Christ and have fellowship with Him. He will teach us the right way to use it.

In my opinion, knowledge is not only connected to insight, understanding, and learning. The Bible opens up another dimension of meaning: It encourages us to recognize God Himself more and more. I would say that after 42 years of marriage, I know my wife pretty well by now – but not only because I know a lot about her, but because I have become consciously engaged with her whole personality. Because of our intimate relationship, I have been able to understand her strengths and weaknesses, her wishes and fears, her goals and her doubts. The same is true in reverse for my wife. In a moment of silence, she once said to me, "You breathe differently. Please tell me what moves you."

Even by the way I breathed, she could tell that something was bothering me. How much more does the Holy Spirit want to lead us into the knowledge of God? Paul writes in the letter to the Ephesians that we are to grow in knowledge to become mature and to be of full age (Eph. 4:13). However, he does not want us to accumulate more theological knowledge, but to understand the divine nature more deeply. Knowledge is not the same as knowing. The mere collection of information might allow me to understand the structure of a piano, but it says nothing about my relationship to music, let alone my ability to play it.

Whoever comes to know God's nature better will also discover himself, for knowledge of God leads to self-knowledge. In His light we see our shadows. In the silence of the encounter with Him, His view of us is revealed. And in His grace, we find forgiveness. God's word is like a mirror for us (Jas. 1:23). Whoever looks into it will not only gain knowledge about God, but also about himself.

The apostle John even goes so far as to directly associate knowledge with love (1 Jn. 4:7f.). We observe a similar connection in the Old Testament: the most intimate moment between a man and a woman is described as "knowledge" (e.g. Gen. 4:1). In general, knowledge is not seen as a purely intellectual process, especially in the Old Testament. The most important organ of knowledge is the heart, with which a person not only feels and senses, but also thinks and understands (e.g. Deut. 8:5; Prov. 18:15). Those who want to grow in spiritual knowledge should cultivate an intimate relationship with God and fall more and more in love with His being - intimately from heart to heart and from spirit to spirit.

The question regarding the gift of the word of knowledge is how we can use it well. Like all the other charisms, it is given for edification (1 Cor. 14:12) – this remains the goal that we should always keep in mind. When I pray for a person who has severe back pain I can also misuse the knowledge gained in prayer to give him unsolicited advice. "You should do more sports! Why do you eat so much? Sitting in front of the computer for so long can't be healthy!" However, such a form of admonition would be neither wise nor encouraging. The impressions that the Spirit gives us should be passed on with respect, patience, and appreciation. When knowledge is combined with love, we will also find the right way to address delicate issues. Because: With a club you can feed a dog or beat it to death. Therefore, knowledge and love should always hold hands. Knowledge will pass away one day, but love endures forever. This is why it continues to be the most important of all gifts (1 Cor. 13:8-13).

8.3 The gift of discerning spirits

In commercial enterprises, risk management is one of the most important tasks of management in modern times. The question of how to detect hazards early and thus avert potential damage plays an enormous role. We are also familiar with early warning systems in everyday life – for example, in road traffic or meteorology. The gift of discerning spirits can be described as a kind of early warning system on a spiritual level. In my view, it is essential for the church. Yet, it is rarely in practice – perhaps because it is so vulnerable to abuse.

The Greek word used in the New Testament for "discernment" is *diakrisis* (1 Cor. 12:10). It can also be translated as "separation", "decision" or "judgment." Paul uses this term frequently in the first letter to the Corinthians. A very well-known passage is found in connection with the words of the institution of the Lord's Supper. There the apostle rebukes certain brothers and sisters who were not able to properly judge the body of Christ and considered it a normal meal (1 Cor. 11:29).

The text shows that discernment means to look at something in a differentiated way, then to examine it, and finally to make a judgment. There is a high degree of responsibility involved in such a task.

It should be noted that this examination in the context of the charism of discernment is not the same as judging the ministry in the spiritual gifts themselves. It is true that the ministry in the spiritual gifts (e.g. prophecy) is to be tested (1 Cor. 14:29; 1 Thess. 5:21).

However, the charism of discernment, in my opinion, is about testing spirits, not Spiritual gifts (though many try to interpret the plural in the word discernments in the way described). It is certainly very helpful if brothers and sisters who evaluate prophecies, for example, also have the gift of discernment. But it is more than that: It is not only a matter of judging whether something is from the Holy Spirit or from man on his own initiative, but whether other spirits are communicating. For the fact is: Not everything that is supernatural comes from God. There is the reality of evil spirits. The Bible does not conceal them and uses the same word for them as for human spirits or the divine spirit: *Pneuma*. Pneuma can stand for all supernatural beings as well as for the inner life of human beings.

IN THE NT REFERRED TO AS THE SPIRIT (PNEUMA)
The Holy Spirit
The spirit of man (e.g. Mt. 26:41; 1 Cor. 2:11)
Good angels (e.g. Heb. 1:14)
Demons or evil spirits (e.g., Mt. 8:16; Acts 19:16).
Princes, mighty ones, world rulers (Eph. 6:12)

Satan is not explicitly referred to as a spirit in the New Testament, but there is no question that he can be counted among the spiritual beings and that he has been understood as such.

Powers of darkness have strength, rule in secret, and even produce miracles. Jesus and his disciples were often confronted with evil spirits working in and through other people. There are many such incidents in the New Testament that we could look at, but that is not the focus of this book. Therefore, I would like to mention just one remarkable experience of Paul's that is worthy of note: When he traveled with his co-workers in Philippi, a fortune-teller ran after them for days, crying out: "These men are servants of the Most High, proclaiming salvation." Although her words were completely true, Paul recognized the spirit of divination in the woman and ordered it to leave her (Acts 16:16-18). She was released on the spot. Apparently, the Holy Spirit had activated a warning system in the apostle and although the woman could not be accused of lying, Paul had good reasons for silencing her. He did indeed cause economic damage to the women's masters, who made their money from fortune-telling, and was punished for it along with Silas. But in the end, this was the lesser of two evils: most likely, he saved the early church from further damage. For if he had acknowledged the word of this woman – where at first glance there was nothing to be said against it – doors would probably have been opened to her as a fortune-teller in Christian circles. Most of the listeners would possibly not have recognized the Trojan horse, if this woman had appeared in a church and had shared her thoughts. Furthermore, by testing the spirits and acting courageously, Paul was able to set the woman straight and thus be of help to her. Paul unmasked the evil Spirit and thus exposed the deceptive cover of the enemy. And he made it clear that God alone should get the glory – not Satan and his demons.

Paul can be a great example for us in this regard: With all sensitivity for the scheming of darkness, I therefore put great emphasis on the importance of the fact that we keep our eyes fixed on Jesus`s victory on the cross.

To him alone belongs the glory. Some time ago, I addressed a person who, in my opinion, was overly focused on the power of evil. I said to the person, «You are giving too much attention to the enemy. That's too much honor for him – Honor he doesn't deserve! Focus on the possibilities of God and not on the battle.» We live and serve in the horizon of God's victory. As Christians we are certainly in the midst of a struggle (Eph. 6:12), but as followers of Jesus Christ we are on the winning side. Therefore, spending too much time with the losing side does not help us very much.

Let us summarize: One who serves in the gift of discerning spirits given by the power of the Holy Spirit should test and discern whether or not God is truly speaking behind a person's word, behavior, or motive.

The discernment can be done on the basis of the following criteria:

- Is God glorified?
- Is Jesus and His redemptive work being magnified?
- Is the Word of God confirmed?
- Is the church being edified?
- Is the individual being brought closer to God?

A person who wants to work with the Holy Spirit in this gift of discernment needs a high degree of spiritual maturity and a deep understanding of the Word of God. Discernment is not based on one's own feelings, personal opinions, or individual preferences. What matters is what God says in the Scriptures or what God reveals through His Spirit. Those who are used to discern the spirits of God should also be willing to share and receive feedback from other gifted people. Acting alone is out of place. None of us can claim to be the only one with the right insight into all contexts. To believe that is the first fallacy. In addition, everyone who serves in the gift of discernment needs to be aware of the fact that judging and condemning are very close to each other.

God does not give his charisms so that we can exalt ourselves above our brothers and sisters and discredit others. He uses his gifts for good purposes. He also wants to bless us with the gift of discernment and build up His church.

The overall testimony of the Bible shows us the reality of the spiritual world and thus also the evil doings of Satan. Out of the darkness he and his demons want to intervene in people's lives and cause destruction. But whoever has given his life to Jesus Christ and walks with Him is on the winning side in this battle, because the Son of God has destroyed the works of Satan (1 Jn. 3:8). Through His death on the cross, He has disempowered the devil and wants to free all who are enslaved (Heb. 2:14f.). The gift of discerning spirits helps the light to continue to triumph over the darkness.

It is not always immediately apparent whether we are dealing with the kingdom of light or the kingdom of darkness, because the devil likes to disguise himself as an angel of light (Mt. 24:24; 2 Cor. 11:14). He is the master of deception. Therefore, church congregations need people who can serve in the gift of discernment. For the testing of spirits requires experience and maturity in faith (Heb. 5:14). Exceptions confirm the rule, but spiritual matters must be judged spiritually. Therefore, spiritual understanding should be present. It is not a matter of making a snap judgment based on feelings, but rather of coming to a well-founded decision after a few steps of testing. I would like to use the following practical example to show what such a process can look like:

4 PHASES OF TESTING

Let's say you are faced with a specific situation in which you are challenged to serve with the gift of discernment. The process of discernment can go through the following four stages:

1. RESTLESSNESS

At first you notice that something is not right. A certain uneasiness rises in you. Maybe you have a picture in your mind's eye or an impression. You may also receive an impulse. In any case, something appears on your spiritual radar screen (e.g. Acts 5:3). You become aware of the command to test the spirits (1 Jn. 4:1). You react to the inner restlessness and become attentive.

2. WEIGHING

Now ask yourself: "Am I sensing a personal feeling here? Or is the Spirit of God really trying to make me aware of something?" A process of inner weighing takes place. At this point, there is a need for caution, for just because something is unusual for you, it does not mean that an evil spirit is active. God's work can also sometimes seem strange to us. He stands above our habits, he is exalted above what we like or what we think is appropriate. Once Jesus came running across the water to His disciples in the boat. No wonder that this occurrence seemed extremely unusual to them. They even thought Jesus was a ghost (Mt. 14:26), but He called out to them that they should not be afraid! Like the disciples, we must not be mistakenly irritated by God's actions.

3. KNOWLEDGE

Now that you have listened carefully and examined the situation with the Word of God, you will come to an inner certainty. It is important, then, that your conclusion be embedded in the interpretive framework of Scripture. If possible, also consult with spiritual leaders or other Christians who are present. This will prevent you from dealing with the matter in isolation and unguarded. The clarity you now have will give you the strength you need to act.

4. CONFRONTATION

You confront the spirit and bring it to light. It is very important on *how* you proceed: The truth should always be told in love (Eph. 4:15). Furthermore, it is not a matter of having manifestations or the evil spirit itself taking center stage. The only important aspect is God`s intention to encourage and admonish through the gift. Affected people must not be exposed in the process. The goal is to win them over and set them straight.

The gift of discerning spirits is not for the purpose of judging situations and people at random. It is about bringing the works of evil to light, so that God gets all the glory and the church of God is built up. Especially in our time, when there is a great interest in spiritualistic and occult powers, we need the gift of discernment the most. This part of the unseen world is foreign to most people in our social environment. The widespread ignorance about it leads to the fact that this side is often completely ignored. As Christians, we are part of society and are in danger of unknowingly adopting its paradigms and thought patterns. This is why Paul also calls on the Romans to renew their minds with a new thinking (Rom. 12:2). With this in mind, I encourage my readers to be aware of the reality of a hostile world. We can boldly reach out to become part of God's spiritual "watchman" and protect what God loves with wisdom and trust in the Lord.

9 THE GIFTS OF POWER

9.1 THE GIFT OF FAITH

In this new chapter, we will now turn our attention to the three gifts of power, as Paul calls them in 1 Corinthians 12: the gift of faith, the gift of healing and the gift of miracles. Before we begin to study the gift of faith, however, it is helpful to look at a brief study that shows the facets in which the Bible speaks of *faith*. In this way, we will gain a better understanding of the term that most of us are familiar with, but which may seem abstract or empty.

The main term for faith used in the Old Testament is the Hebrew word *aman*. This is also the origin of the well-known word "Amen", which means something like "It stands firm" or "So be it". Literally aman means "to stand fast." For example, Genesis 15:6 says, "Abram believed the Lord, and he counted it to him as righteousness." We could also translate: "Abram *made* himself *firm* in the Lord..." The same is true of many other key Old Testament passages that speak of faith (Ex. 4:1-9; Ps. 13:6; Prov. 16:20; Isa. 28:16 and many more). When I read the definition in the Old Testament, I often think of a mountaineer who anchors himself in the rock with a carabiner. He is thereby secured, even if he should slip or fall. In the New Testament the central term for faith is the Greek word *pistis*. It has the basic meaning of "trust." The primary meaning of this word is therefore relationship, not knowledge. Nevertheless, faith (*pistis*) in classical Greek also refers to the intellect. Both aspects are emphasized: the more emotional trust as well as the more rational holding of truth.

That is why the proclamation of the Gospel can also be an appeal to both: the emotions and the intellect!

First of all, let us note that faith in the Bible means an attitude of trust in God. It describes the relationship of a human being to God, which is based on both trust and contemplation. Faith gives stability because it "attaches" itself to God and His word. In the New

Testament, faith unfolds in three additional dimensions, in each of which the Holy Spirit plays a crucial role:

1. FAITH AS THE CONVICTION OF THE HOLY SPIRIT

By hearing the word of God, a person can come to faith (Rom. 10:17; 1 Cor. 15:2, 11; Eph. 1:13; 1 Thess. 2:13). Whoever believes in Christ's death and resurrection receives both the forgiveness of sins and the promise of eternal life (Jn. 3:16-18; Rom. 1:17; 6:8; 10:9; 1 Cor. 15:3-17). This is the faith that saves. Man must accomplish nothing but accept Christ's already completed work.

As indicated earlier, this is a work of the Holy Spirit. He empowers the preacher, reveals the content of the message, convicts the hearer of sin, righteousness, and judgment, and finally takes up residence in the believer.

2. FAITH AS THE FRUIT OF THE HOLY SPIRIT

The Bible, however, does not only talk about people *becoming* believers, but also about *being* a believer. Whether the faith is alive is shown not only in words, but also in deeds (Tit. 3:8; Jas. 1:22; 2:17). Being a believer is not a static state, but rather a dynamic way of life. When I was drafted into the Soviet Air Force, the squadron leader said to me, "Soldier Justus, I have met some people who *talked* about their Christian faith. I will observe whether you really *act* on it."

Much like my old squadron leader, I am convinced that true faith is always visible.

It is not a title that is bestowed on someone, but remains without effect on the person's life. The visible signs of faith are not to be brought about by one's own efforts, but by the power of the Holy Spirit. A tree may be recognized by the rustling of its leaves, but much better by its fruit. Thus, visible faith in the life of a Christian is a fruit of the Holy Spirit (Gal. 5:5). In Galatians, the Greek word *pistis* is usually translated as "faithfulness," because faithfulness is living trust.

My observation is that some Christians are quite strong in their profession of faith, but unfortunately rather weak in their practice. But faith should be practical. It wants to shape us, correct us, change us, motivate us, develop us and much more.

If I tell my wife that I love her, but do not follow up my words with deeds of love, my confession will not be very credible. What is the use of beautiful words for her if they do not become tangible for her in her daily life? In this way, faith without fruit also misses its mark. It should not just be lip service, but action.

3. FAITH AS A CHARISM OF THE HOLY SPIRIT

Finally, in the Bible we find faith as a spiritual gift (1 Cor. 12:9). This faith differs from the previous types, so many authors call it a special faith. Like the other charisms of the Holy Spirit that we have studied so far, this gift is also worked by the Holy Spirit in a selective and situational way. And again, it should be noted that no man can produce such faith on his own. The Holy Spirit must do it. The question arises, however, as to what purpose the special gift of faith is needed at all if a person is already saved by faith and the fruit of the Holy Spirit is constantly increasing in his or her life. To explain this coherence, I would like to point out a remarkable aspect of the gift of faith that becomes clear in the following chapter (1 Cor. 13:2) (in my opinion, Paul is also speaking of faith as a spiritual gift). The apostle obviously characterizes faith as a gift that has the potential to move mountains.

And if I have prophetic powers, and understand all mysteries, and all knowledge, and if I have all faith, so as to remove mountains, but have not love, I am nothing. (1 Cor. 13:2)

Jesus also speaks about faith moving mountains (e.g. Mt. 21:21; Mk. 11:23). It seems that through this charism, the Holy Spirit enables a person to proverbially throw mountains into the sea, that is, to remove obstacles. It is not a matter of making the beautiful Alps disappear, but of overcoming blockages and difficulties in the figurative sense. Through this gift, the Spirit works a pioneering faith: an unshakeable confidence in the effective power of God and a firm expectation of His intervention. This gift comes into play when we can go no further because the way is blocked on all sides. Reasons may include conflict in our personal lives or in the life of the church, challenges at work, financial hardship, illness, and hopeless situations where healing is unlikely. The gift of faith can also be useful in the context of the kingdom of God: When we are challenged to overcome fears and doubts and take a special initiative, such as planting a church in an unfamiliar place; or when courage and motivation are needed in the church for a major project (Acts 27:25).

In the Bible, this special kind of faith appears in various places. James writes that the prayer of faith will save the sick. In this context he mentions the prophet Elijah: He was a man like us. But because he prayed in faith in a specific situation, his prayer was heard (Jas. 5:15-17). Peter, too, once prayed in faith for Tabita, who had already died. God heard his prayer and brought her back to life (Acts 9:40). This kind of faith appears frequently after Pentecost in the book of Acts.

We also know situations, in which mountains tower up before us. But when the Spirit of God works the gift of faith in us, we become capable of moving those mountains. But beware: we cannot simply produce this faith; we have to receive it. It is not a form of positive thinking or the like. Rather, it is the works prepared by God, in which we are to walk (Eph. 2:10). And those who are empowered by the Spirit of God are also commissioned and then expected to respond with obedience.

Many years ago, a person approached me after the service. I was aware of an unpleasant smell of decay in my spirit. Let there be no misunderstanding: The smell did not come from the person, but was literally of a "super-sensual" nature. In that moment, a supernatural faith rose in me. I realized that the Holy Spirit was at work. Without knowing or understanding the person's situation, I recited the text of Psalm 118:17 to the person: "You will not die, but you will live and declare the deeds of the Lord." Deeply moved, the person told me that a medical diagnosis had certified that she would not live much longer. But now she had met someone who walked in the gift of faith. That changed everything. I did not generate this faith myself, but received it from the hand of God. He lets His Spirit blow where and how He wants. I had hesitated fearfully many times before, but in this situation, I courageously said what I had perceived in my spirit. And: This person is still alive today and, as far as I know, healthy. On my journey with the gift of faith, I have also had to learn that my personal condition can deceive me. In some situations, I feel strong in faith, but nothing happens. Other times I feel weak, but God works mightily. Not my feeling determines reality, but the Spirit of God. The faith that He gives can be as tiny as a mustard seed and yet it can bring about great things (Mt. 17:20). Perhaps we could put it this way: Our problem is not that our faith is too little, but that our unbelief is too great!

For by unbelief and doubt we hinder the work of the Holy Spirit. Jesus often criticized the unbelief of his disciples. Therefore, I would say that it is our job to eliminate unbelief. But it is God's part to give us the gift of faith!

Georg Müller is said to have started his orphanage with a few pennies. During the time he ran his orphanage, money was always tight, and at times he had almost nothing left. However, the financial situation was never a reason for him to worry. He always looked up to the Lord and a solution was always found, although he never made an appeal for donations. Through Georg Müller's ministry in faith, several thousand orphans were cared for. Without him, however, his work could not be continued in the same way, for faith cannot be inherited.

9.2 Gifts of Healing

No gift is more sought after by Christians than the gift of healing. At least, this is my personal observation. Since almost every human being or those around them experience sickness and pain, this is hardly surprising.

What is initially striking about the enumeration of this gift in 1Cor. 12:9 is the double plural used in the designation. Paul does not speak of a "healing gift of grace", but of "healing gifts of grace". Incidentally, there is no other text in the New Testament that speaks of someone having the gift of healing. This makes it clear that there is no one clearly defined gift of healing. Instead, there are healing gifts that can be manifested in many ways and with different intensities. Moreover, these gifts do not belong to the person, so that a Christian can call on them at any time to heal the sick at his own discretion. It is God who distributes and activates these gifts according to His will. Thus, as with the other charisms, the gifted person is directly dependent on the Holy Spirit.

The gifts of healing are to be understood as different kinds of spiritual medicine that God's servants give to those in need, as did Peter to the paralytic in Acts 3:6f:

But Peter said, "I have no silver and gold, but what I do have I give to you. In the name of Jesus Christ of Nazareth, rise up and walk." And he took him by the right hand and raised him up, and immediately his feet and ankles were made strong.

The basis for the use of these healing gifts is the situation in which we find ourselves as Christians: On the one hand, we live in a fallen world that is not perfect and therefore has to fight with sickness. On the other hand, God wants to work through His power in this world and bring healing. The overall testimony of the Holy Scripture is clear: Our Creator wants us to be well. He is interested in our total well-being (Ps. 41:4; Ezek. 34:16). Hence it is said:

For I am the Lord who heals you. (Ex. 15:26)

At this point, an important point must be made so that there are no misunderstandings: Just because God fundamentally wants us to be healed does not automatically mean that someone is sick because he has distanced himself from God and His will. Such hypotheses arise because humans tend to look for causes and connections for everything that happens to them. After all, nothing happens without a reason. But do our self-discovered explanations correspond to reality? When it comes to illnesses, some people are quickly tempted to look for the cause in themselves. Some believe that they are not living in the will of the Lord and that this is the reason for their suffering. And indeed, the Bible speaks of the fact that sin and wrongdoing can lead to sickness (1 Cor. 11:30; Jas. 5:15). But this does not lead to the reverse conclusion that a Christian who lives in obedience to God is automatically healthy.

Even though more than a few churches have claimed this in the past, a simple automatic healing for everyone who is a believer does not correspond to the testimony of the Bible, nor to the experience of life: A Christian can live in the center of God's will and still be sick. I have been praying resolutely and courageously for sick people for many years. Many times, I have experienced that God healed people. But as already mentioned, I myself have suffered from allergies for many years. These reactions of my body have natural causes, like most diseases. They are caused by a variety of external circumstances and are and will remain a part of all human life on earth. However, believers are promised the transformation of their bodies into a new resurrection body (e.g. 1 Cor. 15:35-52). Then circumstances will change fundamentally.

But after this brief digression, let us return to the biblical reflection on the work of God for the healing of man. The statements of the Old Testament, in which the Creator reveals Himself as a healer, are intensified in the New Testament with Jesus Christ: A central part of His mission is to heal the sick. In my view, this mission does not relate solely to physical infirmities, nor does it relate solely to mental illness. Jesus seeks the total well-being of man and wants to restore him in every area of life.

It is not the healthy who need a physician, but the sick. (Mt. 9:12)

The Spirit of the Lord is upon me because he has anointed me to proclaim good news to the poor. He has sent me to proclaim liberty to the captives and recovering of sight to the blind, to set at liberty those who are oppressed, to proclaim the year of the Lord's favor. (Lk. 4:18)

Jesus culminates God's work of salvation by giving his disciples the commission of prayer for the sick. It becomes clear that despite his work of redemption on the cross, there will continue to be suffering people for whom, however, various possibilities open up to become healthy:

It is through the ministry of the disciples that people will continue to be healed (Mk. 16:18; Lk. 10:9; Jas. 5:14f.).

The healing intention of God runs like a red thread through the entire Scriptures. It is the basis for our prayers for the sick and causes God to distribute the necessary charisms to do so. Through the gifts of healing brought by the Holy Spirit, God has provided a way for suffering people to be healed. This does not mean, however, that this is always God's only and preferred way.

Disease is multifaceted – in both its causes and its effects. The main reason for this is probably to be found in the fact that, because of the original sin, we are living in a fallen and troubled world. The incident with the blind man in John 9:1-3 shows us that we should not make hasty judgments. In response to the disciples' question whether the sickness was due to the sins of the blind man or the sins of his parents, Jesus' answer is:

It was not that this man sinned, or his parents, but that the works of God might be displayed in him. (Jn. 9:3)

The assumptions made by the disciples reveal the way in which they themselves, as children of their culture, thought about illness. The attitudes of the people of that time toward those who were sick must have been correspondingly prejudiced. Although several thousand years have passed and these clarifying words of Jesus have been handed down to us, Christians today often still think in a similarly sin-centered way when it comes to the suffering of their fellow human beings. But illness is multi-layered. This fact is made clear by the various biblical terms: The Greek word *astheneia* refers to sickness, weakness, and lack of strength of various kinds, and can also have the meaning of transience (Lk. 5:15; Acts 28:9; 1 Cor. 15:43). The word *nosos* is also frequently used and most likely refers to a physical illness caused by a pathogen (Mt. 9:35; Mk. 1:34). The word *malakia* stands for weakness and infirmity (e.g., Mt. 4:23), while the word *kamnoun* refers primarily to mental fatigue and weariness (Jas. 5:15).

As diverse as diseases and their causes are, so are the ways to recovery. Healing in the Bible is not exclusively through spiritual gifts. In Scripture we find the following other ways:

<table>
<tr><td colspan="1">ONE PHYSICIAN – MANY WAYS TO HEALING</td></tr>
<tr><td>Miracles, cloths, shadows (Acts 5:15; 19:2, 1 Cor. 19:12)</td></tr>
<tr><td>Prayer of others in faith (Mk. 11:24; 16:17f)</td></tr>
<tr><td>Anointing with oil, prayer of elders (Jas. 5:14-16)</td></tr>
<tr><td>Personal intercession (Mk. 11:24)</td></tr>
<tr><td>Holy Communion (1 Cor. 11:27-34)</td></tr>
<tr><td>Forgiveness of sins (Jas. 5:16)</td></tr>
<tr><td>Wisdom from the Word of God (Prov. 4:20-23)</td></tr>
<tr><td>Vocational gifts, physicians (1 Pet. 4:10)</td></tr>
<tr><td>Plant Remedies (Jer. 23:15; Isa. 1:6)</td></tr>
<tr><td>Dietary rules (Gal. 5:21)</td></tr>
<tr><td>Own defense mechanisms (Ps. 23:2)</td></tr>
</table>

MIRACULOUS POWERS, CLOTHS, SHADOWS

This form of healing is not a process, but it works immediately and could also be called a miracle. The New Testament provides us with some impressive examples of this. Luke tells us that many healing miracles were performed through the apostles (Acts 5:12). This caused the people to bring the sick outside, so that Peter's shadow would fall on them when he passed by:

...so that they even carried the sick out into the streets and laid them on beds and stretchers, so that when Peter came, at least his shadow would fall on some of them. Many also came

from the surrounding cities to Jerusalem, bringing the sick and those afflicted with unclean spirits, and they were all healed. (Acts 5:15f.)

Luke does not report that people were actually healed by Peter's shadow. At that time, people believed that the shadows of animals or people could transmit healing power or harmful power. Although this idea may seem a little strange to the modern European, the sick were all healed. A similar report about the apostle Paul is handed down to us by Luke in Acts 19:11f.:

And God was doing extraordinary miracles by the hands of Paul, so that even handkerchiefs or aprons that had touched his skin were carried to the sick, and the sicknesses departed from them, and the evil spirits came out of them.

As with the shadows, Luke does not report that the cloths themselves caused the people to be healed. Verse 11 makes it clear, as in other passages, that it is God who works the miracles through the people (e.g., Acts 14:3). So, there were no magical objects. The power of God just seemed to be unlimited. It is also clear that the sick had some kind of saving faith or hope of healing. Just as faith helped the bleeding woman who touched the hem of Jesus' garment (Lk. 8:48), so it would have helped here. The material and "tangible" helped these people connect with God's healing power.

Some time ago, I was ministering in a church for several days and I got to stay overnight with a family. Each time I arrived in the evening, I was given a different room to sleep in. Intrigued, I asked my hosts why they let me sleep in different rooms. "Because we know you pray in the evening. The room and the bed are blessed. That is why you sleep in each of our children's rooms." "According to your faith, let it be as it is for you," I replied to them.

"The effective, fervent prayer of a righteous man avails much, if it is earnest" it is said in Jas. 5:16, regarding prayer for the sick in the church. This statement of James is unmistakable: When believers pray earnestly for one another, it does not remain ineffective. The assurance that people would be healed, when believers pray for the sick, is shown in Mk. 16:17f:

But the signs that will follow those who believe are these: In my name they will cast out demons, speak with new tongues, they will pick up snakes with their hands, and if they drink any deadly poison, it will not hurt them; they will lay hands on the sick, and they will recover.

As we can see, the laying on of hands plays a special role. The laying on of hands is not in itself a magical act that promises a special effect. Similar to the cloths, it can be understood as a faith-strengthening element. It helps the people to imagine a connection between the material world and the invisible world. For me personally, it is important to ask permission before laying hands. Depending on the circumstances, this act may be inappropriate. If it is requested, I treat people respectfully. It is also not always pleasant for the person seeking help to be touched on the head or hair. I prefer the shoulder. If the person I am praying for is downcast, I take his hands from underneath and "support" him or press them slightly upward. In this way, I signal to the person that I support him. In contrast to the "pressure" of the laying on of hands, this approach has a facilitating effect on the recipient of the prayer. The physical touch creates a connection with the person I am praying for.

ANOINTING WITH OIL, PRAYER OF ELDERS

Let us now have a look at the whole passage from James that I quoted in excerpts earlier. James recommends to the believers in the church to turn to the elders in case of sickness and to be anointed with oil:

Is anyone among you sick? Let him call for the elders of the church, that pray over him and anoint him with oil in the name of the Lord. And the prayer of faith will save the sick person, and the Lord will raise him up. And if he has sinned, he will be forgiven. Confess one another your sins and pray for one another that you may be healed. The prayer of the righteous is powerful if it is earnest. (Jas. 5:14-16)

This passage makes it clear that it is not the elders or the oil that guarantee the healing, but "the Lord will raise him up." The mention that they are to pray and anoint in the name of the Lord also clearly suggests this fact. Although the gifts of the Spirit are not available, God seems to stand by the local church leadership and to use them especially in such cases.

I wish that every believer would accept this and call the elders to pray, because when God gives us such a promise, He will also prove to be faithful.

PERSONAL INTERCESSION

Of course, the person in question can also seek the Lord for himself or herself in prayer. It is not only the healing prayer of the brothers and sisters that will be heard. One's own contribution -even if it is obvious – should also be mentioned. In fact, it is important to take the initiative and not just delegate your requests to others. Jesus promised to answer our prayers if they are offered in faith:

Therefore I say to you, whatever things you ask when you pray, believe that you receive them, and you will have them. (Mk. 11:24)

We know that God sees what we need before we ask him (Mt. 6:8). In what way does it still make sense to intercede for oneself? Through the prayer, said in faith, the person reflects on his or her requests and checks whether they are really God's will. The praying person discovers the will of God in prayer. Furthermore, faith incidentally is an expression of trust in God. When Mark writes, "only believe" it means something like "trust your Father in heaven."

THE LORD'S SUPPER

Paul writes to the Corinthians in 1 Cor. 11:27-34 how to behave correctly at the Lord's Supper. He informs the congregation that unworthy participation in the Lord's Supper will result in negative consequences such as sickness. At the same time, the Corinthians were not made sick by the Lord's Supper, but by their unworthy behavior in the Lord's Supper. It is clear from this passage that sin can also make people sick.

Firstly, it is important to note that Paul is not talking about *unworthy people*, but of *unworthy behavior* at the Lord's Supper. "Unworthy" is an adverb that describes the two verbs "to eat" and "to drink" in the text. He is talking about a way of eating and drinking in which the "body of the Lord" is despised. The context shows that he is concerned with inappropriate and unloving behavior in our dealings with one another.

The Lord's Supper in Corinth became a meal where everyone ate and drank what they had brought along, without consideration for others and for the common celebration of the meal, so that some went hungry and others drunk (v. 21). The presence of the Lord in the Lord's Supper was disregarded because the meal was not distinguished from an ordinary "substantial meal", as were the hungry brothers and sisters. Worthy, on the other hand, is a Communion that is characterized by the proper understanding of the Lord's Supper, by brotherly love and the desire to participate in Christ and His church.

In the history of the Protestant churches, Mt. 5:23f. has become the assessment criterion for participation in the Lord's Supper, even though this passage it does not address the participation in the Lord's Supper. The Didache (14:1), which requires confession of sins before the Lord's Supper, may also have played a role. In any case, this tradition is established in many free churches as well. Whoever goes to the Lord's Supper needs to examine whether there is sin between oneself and a brother or a sister. In this passage of the Sermon on the Mount, Jesus demands that the believer first remove his anger toward his brother before fulfilling his obligation to sacrifice. With this, Jesus wants to make it clear that the believer should always be ready to make a fundamental change in his or her attitude toward the neighbor. Reconciliation and love take precedence over the cult of sacrifice. The reconciliation with one`s brother needs to take place before reconciliation with God is possible (e.g., Mt. 6:12, 14; 6:38; Mk. 11:25). Why am I explaining all of this? We recognize that unworthy behavior can make sick. Does worthy behavior then create healing? Some will answer Yes, but Paul is not saying that here. One fact we can see, however, is that reconciliation and love in the Church *prevent* disease. The Lord's Supper repeatedly reminds us that love is important to keep brothers and sisters from falling sick. I also believe that a community characterized by mutual appreciation and love for one another is a place where people can be healed. Furthermore, our Lord meets us in the Lord's Supper. It is not only a meal of remembrance, but also a meal of communion with the Lord. The encounter with our Lord has a transforming power. In this respect, the Lord's Supper has a special meaning when we talk about healing.

FORGIVENESS OF SINS

As we have just seen, God's forgiveness is linked to our own forgiveness. In the prayer that our Lord taught us we pray: "And forgive us our debts, as we forgive our debtors" (Mt. 6:12). Our forgiveness presupposes, so to speak, the forgiveness of God. We have also seen that reconciliation and fraternal love are more important to God than the cult of sacrifice (Mt. 5:23f.). It is not surprising, therefore, that James, in the passage we have already considered, urges us to confess our sins to one another so that we may be healed (Jas. 5:16). Obviously James believed that forgiveness of sins was necessary in order to be healed of sickness. The fact that every obstacle is removed between people and before God plays an important role in healing. In addition, we see in James that interceding for one another should take place only after everything has been cleared up. It is not clear whether this means confessing one's sins to the other, or whether it means confessing sins in general. In any case, guilt is a burdensome power and must go to the cross. When guilt or anything else comes between people, it has a negative effect, as we have just seen in the communion text. It is as if a burden has been placed on the person. Not only the psyche, but also the body can be affected.

I have heard of interesting incidents: A clergyman prayed for a person who had severe back pain. The person seeking advice said that he had sins to confess. In prayer the clergyman got an impulse, which he immediately passed on: "Buy yourself a new mattress. Your old mattress is worn out." A physical burden is not always in connection with sin, but it can be, as in the second example: The other person the pastor prayed for had stomach problems. Again, the praying man responded in an interesting way: "The stomach is not only related to food. You have anger and unforgiveness in your stomach that is causing this pain." Tolerated unforgiveness can cause disease if there is no repentance in the person.

Wisdom from the Word of God

That the Bible is good for the human soul is certainly known and plausible. The Holy Scriptures make it clear that God loves and is for man. It contains many comforting and uplifting words, so it is understandable that it gives healing to the human soul. The Bible also reports that healing of the human body takes place when one acts wisely:

My son, be attentive to my words; incline your ear to my sayings. Do not let them escape your sight; keep them in your heart, for they are life to those who find them and healing to their whole body. Guard your heart with all diligence, for life springs from it. (Prov. 4:20-23)

The wisdom teaching of the Holy Scriptures is something precious that should not be ignored when dealing with healing.

VOCATIONAL GIFTS, DOCTORS

Although God has healed people throughout history, the Bible does not speak against the abilities of physicians. Sometimes I hear Christians say that we as Christians do not need a doctor or medicine, because the Lord is our physician. I like to respond with the following answer: "Then you must not wear glasses or go to the dentist." We can be thankful for doctors and physicians of all specialties. They study our bodies to understand how they work, and they look for ways to put the body back together when something is not right. This is good and we should make use of it. After all, these people have good gifts, so there is nothing wrong with them using them (1 Pet. 4:10). When I was 19 years old, I had my appendix removed. Thank God I had the surgery, because if it had not happened, I probably would not be alive today.
Our bodies are subject to natural wear and tear, and diseases and ailments come upon us as we age. This is inevitable for us, because in the long run our place is not in in this world. Solomon already knew this and wrote in Ecclesiastes 12:2-4:

That is when the light of the sun, the moon, and the stars will grow dim for you, and the rain clouds will never pass away. Then your arms, that have protected you, will tremble, and your legs, now strong, will grow weak. Your teeth will be too few to chew your food, and your eyes too dim to see clearly. Your ears will be deaf to the noise of the street. You will barely be able to hear the mill as it grinds or music as it plays, but even the song of a bird will wake you from sleep.

PLANT REMEDIES

The Bible mentions over 100 plants. Some of them are used as images, such as the grapevine. Others are used for food. And it speaks of plants with healing powers. Our Lord and Creator placed healing agents in creation. Plants serve us not only for food, but also for healing.

There are always believers who object to herbal remedies, but we see throughout the Bible that people used herbal remedies for medical purposes (cf. Jer. 23:15; Isa. 1:6; 38:21; 1 Tim. 5:23; Rev. 22:2).

DIETARY REGULATIONS

It is well known that poor diet can lead to many diseases. For example, excessive consumption of sugar or meat can be harmful. Therefore, it is advisable to pay attention to your diet.

Paul is harsh with people who eat too much food:

...envyings, murders, drunkenness, revellings, and such like: of the which I tell you before, as I have also told you in time past, that they which do such things shall not inherit the kingdom of God. (Gal. 5:21)

This verse is rarely mentioned in connection with sickness. Eating in itself is not bad, but Paul associates overeating with other sins. As with all things it depends on the quantity. Overeating has a bad effect - not only on our bodies. Therefore, it is obvious why Paul is so critical of it.

The Bible knows a series of dietary rules in both the Old and the New Testament, which I will not elaborate on at this point. Paul does not see following of any dietary laws as necessary for salvation:

I know and am certain in the Lord Jesus that nothing is unclean in itself; only to him who considers it unclean. (Rom. 14:14)

This does not mean, of course, that some dietary rules cannot be helpful. The Jews, for example, have a special way of separating their food. This is not related to food combining itself. For example, they do not eat dairy products in combination with meat. After several visits to Israel, my wife Irene and I realized that we no longer eat meat in the morning either. Our eating habits have changed because of this different culture, and that is not a bad thing. It would not hurt if other people adopted different eating habits as well. An illness that is the result of a less-than-optimal diet will probably not be prayed away, but will require a change in eating habits.

OWN DEFENSE MECHANISMS

Our creator has made our body in a great way. God has given the body the ability to initiate certain healing processes when it is weakened or sick. In such a case, medicine has a good contribution to make in supporting these processes. Medicine in itself does not always heal, but supports or enables the healing process.
Sometimes you need to be aware of this fact and allow for times of renewal. In Psalm 23 we see that God our Shepherd leads us as His sheep to places of renewal:

He feeds me in green pastures and leads me to fresh waters.
(Ps. 23:2)

As you can see, we have a pharmacy of God within us. At the same time, we have a mandate to support this pharmacy, for example, by strengthening our body's defenses. It is not for nothing that we are told: "The greatest physician is within us."
Around 1997, my wife Irene experienced a physical and mental breakdown and fell into a severe stress-related depression. We immediately sought the Lord and begged Him repeatedly for healing. Friends and fellow believers in our congregation and beyond joined us in prayer. I longed to experience God's work through a gift of healing. But in the end, we had to admit to ourselves that ill-

nesses cannot simply be prayed away and that healing comes about through many complementary methods and ways. Irene had to change her lifestyle, some habits and her diet. She was challenged to learn to say No and to set limits early on. It became clearer and clearer that it was not an attack from the enemy that was responsible for her condition, but that our lifestyle had contributed to this serious breakdown.

My wife finally took a health cure, sought medical help, followed doctors' advice and took medication. All these different aspects together helped Irene to begin her journey of recovery. How many times I've sincerely wished for a spontaneous healing and asked God for it. But instead, I was reminded of Ecclesiastes 12, which laments growing old and weak. I had to learn that all of our strength, knowledge, and wisdom are just bits and pieces.

In the end, we are all dependent on God, who works through His Spirit as He wills – not as we expect.

We received more spiritual and practical support from other people than ever before, which also contributed greatly to Irene`s recovery. A lady from church, for example, came regularly to help us with the house chores. When my wife began to complain: "My soul sings no more. My body cannot carry on any longer. My faith no longer sustains." others replied, "We are singing for you now. We are working for you now. We are believing for you now." I believe the value of cohesion and community is underestimated in alleviating people's suffering (1 Cor. 12:26; Gal. 6:2). Often people are the extended arm of God working in healing.

One day, one of my sons came to see me to ask for advice. It was about some people around him who needed help. "They need a miracle!" he stated. I confirmed his words, but I felt that I should add something else: "Right. You be the miracle." He was visibly challenged, but understood the implication.

I wish that the charisms of healing would be used much more in our churches. But I also know that we can become unbalanced by a one-sided emphasis on spiritual gifts. Therefore, we must take into account the many different methods of healing that we find in the

Bible. In the end, it is not the perfect method that is important, but rather that we look for ways in faith and trust in God to bring salvation to people. Our relationship with Him gives us strength and wisdom.

SERVING IN THE GIFTS OF HEALINGS - TWELVE PRACTICAL TIPS

After some basic reflections on sickness and ways of restoration, I would now like to offer twelve practical recommendations for all those who want to serve in a healing gift of grace.

1. *Seek to be close to God:* Before God works through you, he wants to work in you. Therefore, cultivate your relationship with God and let Him shape, mold, and transform you. Grow in the knowledge of His word and be filled with His power.

2. *Strive for the healing gifts of grace:* Tell God that you want to be blessed with the gifts of healing and want to serve in them. Reach out for this blessing that Jesus promised to His church. Remember - it is not first and foremost about you. As with any other gift, God desires to build up the church through the gifts of healing. Therefore, look for situations and opportunities to serve. Be bold, but do not frantically try to make things happen on your own or in overconfidence. I emphasize again: God's Spirit distributes as He wills (1 Cor. 12:11).

3. *Develop a sense for the sick:* Jesus was able to meet people in their distress, because he was deeply moved by their suffering. Those who want to serve the sick need interest, compassion, and understanding of their concerns. Therefore, sharpen your eyes for the world of the suffering and be ready to engage in their situations.

4. *Do not focus on the afflictions, but on the human being:* God does not just want to heal the disease, He wants to restore the whole person. When I was taking a health cure for my back problems, I liked the following statement from a doctor: «We do not treat the disease, but the person.» When you serve a person, don't define them by their afflictions. Look at the person that is in front of you.

5. *Share the Gospel:* Gifts of healing often reveal themselves in a missionary context. This is evident from the Bible as well as from the testimonies of past and present church history. Where the Gospel is preached, God often confirms His word through signs and wonders (Acts 2:43; 3:3ff.; 14:3). So proclaim the good news to people who have not yet heard it – and then pray boldly for their sicknesses!

6. *Pray in word and deed: Not only the clear, precise wording, but sometimes also a symbolic action, such as the laying on of hands, can be helpful in a prayer for healing (Mk. 16:18) – of course only if it is requested.*

7. *Do not be irritated by your perceptions or thoughts:* Sometimes I know for sure that the power of God is present. At other times I feel nothing at all or I even have doubts and people are touched anyway. We should pray for the sick regardless of our feelings. God's power is at work – whether we feel it or not is not the deciding factor.

8. *Let the Holy Spirit lead you:* Listen to the voice of God and His words. Be aware of His impulses. Allow Him to guide you in prayer, for it does not depend on you, but on Him.

9. *Encourage people to live wise lives:* After healing the sick man at the pond of Bethesda Jesus said to him, «Sin no more.» (Jn. 5:14). Those who have been healed should then live in such a way that they remain healthy. Often the sick person has also caused his own miserable condition. In the same way, he should now contribute to his health by living wisely.

10. *Point out the various ways of healing:* Health comes in many ways, including forgiveness of sins, God's power, and prayer directly, as well as through medical treatment, medication, a healthy diet, adequate exercise, and rest. Point out these ways to the recipient of the prayer so that he or she will not become rigidly attached to only one way of doing things. Also, remember that you are not a doctor unless you have training in that area. So be careful about giving explicit medical advice. It is not our responsibility to decide whether or not to keep taking medication. A specialist should be consulted.

11. *Motivate the use of companionship:* Because healing can be a process, we need people to journey with us. Encourage the sick person to commit to joining a Christian community. There is power in believers supporting one another (Gal. 6:2).

12. *Strengthen the trust in God:* While not every prayer will make an immediate or visible difference, it should encourage and increase confidence and faith. As you pray together, focus on the possibilities and promises God has given. In this way, fear and worry must give way. God's peace can fill and strengthen a person in spite of illness.

HOW TO PRAY FOR THE SICK

In prayer, we can simply ask the Lord for healing. It is not a matter of a special formula, but of the person praying simply speaking from his own heart. The expectation of healing should be reasonable. It is not written: "The prayer of the righteous can do all things." But rather, "...is able to do much." (Jas. 5:16). Ultimately, God is the healer, not us. This attitude protects both sides from catastrophes of faith. At the same time, this certain level-headedness should not lead us to not pray at all. In the gospel of Mark we read that those who are weak are made well when those who follow Jesus lay hands on them (Mk. 16:18). We are called to follow suit.

Similarly, it is written of the elders of the church that they should anoint the sick with oil (Jas. 5:14). I wish that every believer would accept this offer and call the elders to him for prayer. For when God gives us a promise, He will be faithful. At this point, those who preside over the church are specifically mentioned, but this does not mean that anyone else is forbidden to anoint with oil. This gesture can accompany prayer as well.

The gifts of healing are often accompanied by prophetic words. I was able to experience this, among other things, when the Holy Spirit worked through me for the first time with a charism of healing: A terminally ill person, who according to medical information had only 14 days to live, called me and asked me to come. I agreed at short notice. On the morning of the day of the visit, I woke up with the inner certainty that I should go there and say to the person "Be rid of the disease and you shall live!". I explained to the person that I was going to pray in tongues for a period of time as well as lay my hands on him. The person had no experience with this, but was fine with it. After about a quarter of an hour I said "You shall live!". Some time later I met this person again who was now completely healthy and ready to tell others about Jesus!

9.3 THE GIFT OF POWER EFFECTS

Now we come to the third charism in the bundle of power gifts: the "gift of power effects". Some of us may find it rather difficult to imagine anything explicit under these effects of power. Some Bible translations use the term "gift of miracles". This does not necessarily enhance a better understanding though. The term I have used here as "gift of power effects" may also be a bit misleading – because what we have already noticed in the basic Greek text in 1 Cor. 12:10, we observe again: that Paul uses a double plural. He literally speaks of "effects of powers" (*energemeta dynameon*).

This term does not sound like a precise description of the gift, since the effects and powers can be manifold. Moreover, we search in vain for a more detailed description of Paul's content. So we can hardly grasp what kind of effect is meant here. For some this may be a disadvantage, but for me it is quite positive:

 Paul obviously avoids limiting the gift to certain forms of manifestation – after all, the power of the Holy Spirit is manifested in many ways (1 Cor. 12:6). It would not do justice to its nature to draw up a static catalogue of possible effects.

Even when power or miracles are mentioned elsewhere in the New Testament, it is usually not clear what exactly is meant: Acts 2:22 talks about Jesus' signs and miracles – but without further explanation. The same is true of Romans 15:18f. where Paul speaks of his own ministry. In addition, the writer of Hebrews simply describes various miracles that confirm the gospel of Jesus Christ without giving any further explanation or details about the miracles.

While God also bore witness by signs and wonders and various miracles and by gifts of the Holy Spirit distributed according to his will. (Heb. 2:4)

This open formulation invites us not to become narrow in our thinking, but to keep a broad heart. For those who have a preconceived notion of the effects of power also allow it only to a limited extent. But just as life is diverse in its challenges, so are the "wonderful" answers that the Spirit wants to give us.

One thing, however, can always be said about the gift of power effects in whatever form it may appear: its manifestations go beyond what we would call normal and ordinary. This definition may sound somewhat trivial and yet it hits the essential core: What seems to be astonishing to us is a standard for God. And what seems supernatural to us is quite natural for God. When it comes to the effects of God's power, we must be prepared to recognize and accept the work of God. This emphasis is all the more necessary because even Christians are closed to many things that are unknown and unfamiliar to them. But this should not be the case!

God has chosen to work in miraculous ways: When Jesus turns water into wine or instantly heals a lame man who has been paralyzed for decades, it is a creative act that goes beyond the normal and ordinary. When I pray for a cancer patient who simultaneously receives a completely new, healthy and functioning esophagus, we are obviously dealing with an instantaneous miracle, not a process of healing.

The report in Acts 5:12-15, according to which the sick were healed simply by being touched by the shadow of Peter that fell on them, also goes far beyond the natural. The acts of power of the apostle Paul in Acts 19:11-12 are even literally said to be no ordinary acts of power:

And God was doing extraordinary miracles by the hands of Paul, so that even handkerchiefs or aprons that had touched his skin were carried away to the sick, and their diseases left them and the evil spirits came out of them.

Such acts of deliverance and even raising of the dead (e.g., in Acts 20:7-12) are also to be mentioned when speaking of power effects. The rapture of Philip from Gaza to Ashdod (Acts 8:39-40) is also described as a supernatural work of the Holy Spirit.

From my point of view, it is exactly such events that Paul is referring to when he talks about the gift of power effects. The Holy Spirit works as powerfully today as he did then, and miracles of all kinds happen: There are psychological and physical phenomena, demon exorcisms, instantaneous healings, natural miracles, weather changes, creation miracles, and much more.

My wife, Irene, once experienced a physical power effect of God: At a women's conference, the speaker proclaimed that she would be healed of her chronic migraines. The pain was not only gone immediately, it never came back – and that was 24 years ago!

Through the gift of power effects, we become attentive to the power of the Holy Spirit, which exceeds our limited possibilities. It helps us humans to see beyond our own horizons. We can trust God to do the impossible! Certainly, what we wish for and reality often differ. That is why I encourage you to be on the lookout not for the reality of our own desires, but for the effective reality of the Holy Spirit. When I read about the gift of power effects in the Scriptures, I want to trust that God's Word will prove to be true. I don't just want to read it, I want to let it work in power.

I would like to emphasize one important aspect at this point, and that is the center to which the power effects point. As the writer of the Letter to the Hebrews makes clear, signs and wonders keep our focus on the main thing: the Gospel (Heb. 2:4). We also find other passages that reveal this indicative character of the gifts of power. Jesus sent the disciples to heal the sick and proclaim the kingdom of heaven (Lk. 9:2; 10:9). These and other Bible accounts illustrate how the message of the kingdom of God was accompanied by signs and wonders when Jesus and his disciples were among the people. Like signposts, the Spirit's power effects point to something important rather than to themselves: God uses signs and wonders to make it clear that He Himself is at work in the proclamation of the Gospel. With Jesus, the kingdom of God has already begun and is present (cf. ch. 6). However, according to New Testament statements, it will be fully realized only in the last days. It is therefore not yet present in its full extent. So signs and wonders confirm the reality of the kingdom of God. And they allow us to get a glimpse of what it is going to be like when the kingdom of God has come in its fullness. This encourages me. It inspires my anticipation of Jesus' return and the full unfolding of His reign on earth. Therefore, as a participant in the kingdom already in the making, I strive to have the gift of power effects at work in the proclamation of the Gospel.

I continue to ask myself how I can personally contribute to making this gift a reality in my ministry.

I have noticed that I am quick to pray for a miracle when I am in a hopeless situation. In doing so I spare no effort, show perseverance, and persistence. The main reason for my great motivation is probably the fact that I am personally affected. The gift of power effects, on the other hand, is for my neighbor. The Holy Spirit wants to meet other people in their distress through His supernatural intervention, just as Jesus used to do when He walked on earth. In this way, people come into contact with the kingdom of God and can immediately respond to it. When I think of this, it encourages me to pray for this gift with the same zeal I just described. The fact that power effects were manifest and obviously necessary in the early church makes me realize that they must still be significant and necessary today.

However, God's kingdom never passes into our hands. It remains – as the word itself says – *His* kingdom. Therefore, no Christian can work miracles out of his own strength. God is the one who does His work in man – sometimes directly, sometimes with the help of a third person. And even when the work of power is done through a human being, this third person is actively involved in God's will by acting in faith.

But what can we personally do to become such a "third person"? In the following, I would like to offer some suggestions:

- We should ask and long to be used by God (according to 1 Cor. 14:1).
- Being close to God helps us to become sensitive to what God wants to do.
- Those who have a heart for the needs of others will find it easy to be used by God to work miracles in the lives of others.
- It really is possible for God to do miracles through us. We can count on it.

If we keep these points in mind, we will remain in an active state of expectation, with eyes open to what God wants to do.

We have seen in Scripture that signs and wonders followed Jesus and the apostles. Unfortunately, I have observed for years that it is exactly the opposite with some Christians: They run after signs and wonders – which, sadly, do not follow them at all. Personally, I have decided not to run after miracles, but to strive for my own life to be accompanied by the effects of power. I am not doing this for the sake of the manifestations, but for the sake of the people that God wants to reach with the message of salvation. I can only encourage each of us to make such a decision.

In this context, before closing, I would like to pass on an impressive life story. It is a testimony to how God works miracles in a person's life. The lady who is the subject of this story has given me permission to publish it here:

My story begins in a small village in the middle of Germany. I grew up in a normal family, with a father, a mother and a little sister. As children of the post-war era, my parents had made it their business to give us a happy childhood. I, too, would have had a happy childhood had it not been for the abuse I suffered at the hands of my uncle. This guilt became our "family secret".

That there was a God in heaven was clear to me as a child, but that I could have a personal relationship with my Creator through Jesus

Christ was something I did not understand in my younger years. I loved the stories of Jesus that I heard in confirmation class, but I did not understand why He had to die on the cross. It was not until later that I received the revelation.

As a teenager, I was raped several times. Gone was my dream of keeping myself pure for my future husband. I felt inferior, dirty, and ugly. Who would want me now? At regular intervals, I had to have cysts and lumps removed from my lower abdomen. I was in a lot of pain and often had to call in sick during my training.

It was around this time that I met my husband. It was like a dream: As he walked through the door, I heard a voice in my ear saying, "This is your husband." We both realized that we belonged together and that we would go through life together. There was just one catch: He was from the hooligan scene, very hurt and full of violence. I, on the other hand, was a woman without any self-esteem. But together we set out on a search for God.

Things seemed to get even more complicated when, in the fall of 1985, after another operation, the university clinic confirmed that I was 99 percent infertile. The next dream was shattered: the hope of having children one day. I began to cry out to God with all my heart: "If you really exist..." Three months later, I was expecting our first son.

My gynecologist was speechless. But that was only the first miracle we experienced: in 1987, eleven months after the birth of our son, we held our baby daughter in our arms. Again, my doctor could not believe it. But we knew the Lord was at work to fulfill our heart's desire. In 1988, our second son was born. That was the moment I began to talk to my gynecologist about God and His intervention in my life. He was very moved and at a loss for words.

We went to Bible school with three children, and in 1991 another daughter was entrusted to us. At that time we had already received the call of God to the mission field in Western Europe. Last but not least, the Lord gave us another girl in 1993.

Through Jesus Christ, I was able to forgive my uncle and the other men who had abused me and taken away my dignity. In fact, I was even able to bless them and ask the Lord that they too would come to know the Savior as well. No more cysts or lumps were ever found in my lower abdomen and my pain was finally a thing of the past.

Today, my husband and I are looking back on 30 years of marriage. For 25 years we have been on the mission field in Western Europe - and now even beyond. But the most beautiful gift for me is the fact that all of our children know and love Jesus and that we are in ministry together with four of them.

It is good to trust God, to listen to Him and to follow His instructions. I am happy to have been able to pray with and accompany many victims of abuse in their journey of healing and restoration over the past years. Today I can say with all my heart: All things work together for good to those who believe.

10 Language gifts

10.1 The gift of tongues

Speaking in tongues – an indication of the baptism in the Spirit?

Let us now turn to the third category of spiritual gifts, the so-called language gifts (speaking in tongues and prophecy). The gift of speaking in tongues is probably the charism that is discussed in the most controversial way. The gift of tongues is, in a way, a «problem child» – if nothing else, because it is often unfavorably associated with the baptism in the Spirit. In some circles this is still the case today. Speaking in tongues is considered «*initial evidence*». This term (especially among American brothers and sisters) stems from the conviction that speaking in tongues is an indicator of the baptism in the Holy Spirit. In Germany, on the other hand, a rethinking has taken place.

In this regard, I would like to state at the outset that we do not get a set of rules from the Lucan accounts as to how the baptism in the Spirit should explicitly manifest itself. Only one fact is clear from Acts, namely that it was always accompanied by perceptible signs: The baptism in the Spirit was generally accompanied by tongues (Acts 2:4; 10:46; 19:6), but also by power effects (4:31), prophecy (19:6), and praise (2:11; 10:46; 11:15). Acts 8:17f. also mentions the baptism in the Holy Spirit, but the account doesn't give any details about what kind of manifestations were present. It merely says that certain signs were visible.

The apostle Paul states in 1 Cor. 12:27-30 that not every believer has all the gifts:

«Do all possess gifts of healing? Do they all speak with tongues?

Do all interpret?» (1 Cor. 12:30)

The apostle's question here is purely rhetorical and must be answered with a resounding «no.»[16] This would be a misinterpretation of his statement, for the gift of tongues, like all the others, is sovereignly given by the Spirit of God. If he had meant to say that all Christians receive this gift, he would not have mentioned it here. But the apostle consciously includes it here. Indeed, there is a theory that Paul is not talking about speaking in tongues, which believers receive when baptized with the Spirit, but about speaking in another way. In my view, however, it is not plausible to split the gift of tongues into two different gifts (for that is what we would have to do if we took Paul seriously here and wanted to hold on to the conviction that every Christian receives the gift of tongues at the baptism in the Spirit). The proponents of this theory usually refer to the following verse:

Now I want you all to speak in tongues, but even more to prophesy. The one who prophesies is greater than the one who speaks in tongues, unless someone interprets, so that the church may be built up. (1 Cor. 14:5)

Paul's desire that all would speak in tongues is correctly translated, but in my opinion it does not reflect the real concern that the apostle is expressing here: He would like to see all Christians praying in tongues. If it were up to him, the entire church would be able to do so. However, he considers it far more desirable that all minister in the prophetic (1 Cor. 14,5; 24f.). We must not conclude from Paul's desire for everyone to pray in tongues that everyone has received this gift – especially since he himself points out in 1 Corinthians 14:23 that it can be counterproductive for everyone to speak in tongues at the same time.

------

16 *The verses in 1 Corinthians 12:29-30 contain seven rhetorical questions, all of which must be answered «no» according to Greek grammar.*

In principle, I am in complete agreement with Paul's opinion. It is also my desire that all believers have the gift of tongues. I believe that the gift is theoretically available to everyone.

Nevertheless, this does not mean that everyone does speak in tongues. The reasons for this vary: Some receive the gift of tongues, but do not practice it. They neglect it, such as Timothy (2 Tim. 1:6). As a result, it gradually loses its presence in their life of faith.

TYPES OF SPEAKING IN TONGUES

With this introductory discussion, we now come to another central aspect of speaking in tongues. When we look at *glóssa* – the corresponding term in the original Greek text – we already encounter some peculiarities in the translation: The word can mean both the tongue and language. For this reason alone, there are various names for this gift, such as, «prayer in languages», «speaking in languages» or «speaking in tongues». All of these are legitimate and in common use. Moreover, Paul again uses a double plural when he speaks of «kinds of tongues» and not just of a «gift of tongues». I think this also indicates that speaking in tongues can manifest itself in different ways.

The following table outlines the different types of tongues for a first overview.

Different types of speaking in tongues
Earthly languages (Acts 2:4, 6)
Worship (Jn. 4:23; Acts 10:44-46; 1 Cor. 14:15)
Prayer of thanksgiving (1 Cor. 14:16f.)
Intercessory prayer (Rom. 8:26)
Act of authority (Mk. 16:17)
Means for one's own edification (1 Cor. 14:1-4)
Prophetic speaking in tongues

We encounter a first form in Acts 2:4, 6:

And they were all filled with the Holy Spirit, and began to speak in other languages as the Spirit inspired them. And at this sound the multitude came together, and they were bewilderd, because each one was hearing them speak in his own language.

The terms used here clearly show that on the one hand the gift of tongues is expressed in *actually existing earthly languages*. However, it can also be languages that are not of earthly origin (1 Cor. 13:1). Especially in chapter 14, it becomes clear that speaking in tongues is first and foremost a private prayer addressed to God (1 Cor. 14, 2, 4, 14, 28). Thus, it is probably the only gift of the Spirit that is not primarily given to encourage and strengthen the church, but to build up the individual. But the one who is strengthened can more easily do good to others. In this sense, speaking in tongues ultimately serves the body of Christ as a whole.

In the chapter that is particularly important on the subject of tongues, 1 Corinthians 14, the verb «to speak» occurs 24 times - more than in any other chapter of the New Testament! This in turn

Part 3: Serving in the grace of God | **139**

opens our eyes to the fact that the Spirit of God wants to work in a special way through verbal communication. The miracle that takes place in a person with the gift of tongues becomes especially clear when we consider what it takes to learn a foreign language. It takes not only talent, but also a great deal of time, effort, and discipline. In comparison, speaking in tongues is a gift of God that cannot be learned. With it, we are given the opportunity to express ourselves in a language that is chosen by the Holy Spirit Himself.

Sometimes, as a prayerful person, I may realize that certain things are happening in secret for which I have no words. In such a case, I can rely on God to give me the right words. Therefore, I often ask people with whom I would like to come to God for permission to pray in tongues first.

In this way, I personally build up and bless people at the same time. Time and time again, I experience God showing me what I am praying for at that moment, and my impression is confirmed in the subsequent conversation with the person.

I am very grateful for this kind of communication and its diversity. As was made clear at the beginning, speaking in tongues can also occur in several other forms, including *worship* – to name just one more as an example. Personally, I am not considered a gifted worship singer, but some time ago my neighbor told me in the elevator that she liked my singing. She said to me, «You sing so beautifully.» These are not actual songs, but rather prayers and songs that I sing in tongues in my office. I think she picks up on that and finds it appealing. So speaking in tongues can also be a prayer of thanksgiving and worship, and I benefit a lot from it.

All in all, I believe that speaking in tongues is the most controversial of all the spiritual gifts. All the more reason to remember the blessing it can bring to the church and to the individual. Moreover, it is remarkable that the praying person cannot sin with this heavenly language. Our human language is brutalized, distorted by all kinds of strong language, and stained by all the evil words with which we have already done harm. None of this can happen with the languages of the Holy Spirit.

Now that we have had a look at some types of speaking in tongues, there is one thing we can say: The recipient determines the form of speaking in tongues. All of the types I have discussed so far are addressed to God. When we pray in tongues – alone or with others – we are always calling on God. No one else needs to understand it except the one to whom it is addressed (1 Cor. 14:2). The same is true of singing in tongues. Here, too, the person is directing his praise to God. Compared to praying together in tongues, singing seems harmonious and almost orderly.

Therefore, it is not surprising that this form of speaking in tongues is more often used in church services, especially because of the guests attending the service.

But in addition to all the forms addressed to God, there is also a place for another kind of tongue: the tongue addressed to man. It must necessarily be accompanied by another gift - the gift of interpretation. Only then can the church benefit from the foreign words of the Spirit. Because this gift is so closely related to the gift of tongues, I want to include it in this chapter.

INTERPRETATION OF TONGUES

Paul writes a few lines later in 1 Cor. 14:1 that this kind of public speaking in tongues should not remain incomprehensible to the people: «...whoever speaks in tongues, pray that he may also interpret it...». Therefore, I would encourage all of us to strive to make what is said as accessible as possible to all. It is not to be condemned to speak in new tongues and not to receive an interpretation in the process. But we must not forget: This spiritual gift (like all others) is also given for the edification of our fellow men and can serve them, especially if they understand what is being said!

My own baptism in the Spirit was accompanied by prophetic words and revelations. The gift of speaking in tongues, however, I did not receive until about four days later – while I was mucking out the stable! For hours I praised the Lord in other tongues. Pragmatic as she is, my wife came up to me and asked: «Why don't you interpret what was said? After all, that's what the Scriptures say, isn't it?» That was the beginning of my prayer for the gift of interpretation (1 Cor. 12:10). Today I receive more frequent revelations about what I am praying in other tongues.

It is noteworthy in this context that the term «edification» runs through the entire fourteenth chapter of First Corinthians, thus becoming the central idea (vv. 3, 4, 5, 12, 17 u. 26).

We must keep this in mind and direct our actions accordingly: How can I edify my brother or sister by speaking in an incomprehensible language? I must see to it that someone interprets the words so that what is said reaches the recipient.[17] If I cannot ensure this, then I should rather keep silent (1 Cor. 14:28).

But how does the individual know if there is someone who can interpret the message, if he does not possess the gift of interpretation himself?

Our conclusion from the biblical text is that the church leadership was aware of the gift profiles of the individuals in the church and was able to address them in the context of the situation. It follows that this gift – like any other – should be exercised in coordination with the leadership of the church. These thoughts are the basis for the questions we want to address in the next section: How can praying in tongues work in the church service? Should we practice it at all? And what opportunities and challenges do we face along the way?

PRAYING IN TONGUES IN THE CHURCH SERVICE – OPPORTUNITY AND CHALLENGE

Personally, I am a proponent of singing in tongues and semi-loud praying in tongues in public meetings – as long as it is done in an orderly fashion. For we see in the New Testament that even tongues must have been heard by the brothers and sisters in the early church:

---

17 The «interpretation» of tongues, Greek hermeneia, means something like «explanation», but much more simply «translation». However, since it is not an activity of the mind, the association with the work of an interpreter should be avoided.

...for they heard them speak with tongues and magnify God. (Acts 10:46)

The individual is not disturbed because he is focused on his personal dialogue with God. It is the same when I hear that many people around me are praying. And even more: It is actually conducive to my prayer because I have the feeling that I am part of the whole and that I am carried along. Therefore, it makes perfect sense for all of us to pray or sing at the same time in our meetings – in German or in tongues. In this way, we do not have to wait until one person has had their turn in prayer. However, because in our culture praying in this way is perceived as chaotic, I recommend singing in tongues together in public church services. Praying loudly together in tongues unfortunately often leads to complaints. Some people believe that they are especially spiritual if they pray extra loud and want to be perceived as such. It is ergo not uncommon for a competition to develop between brothers and sisters who shout loudly in tongues. Others feel that they must make noise through the microphone in the direction of the congregation. But as long as there is no one available to interpret what is being said, this is unproductive and the praying person should actually remain silent.

As a matter of principle, it should be noted here that there is no mention of ecstatic babbling or trance states into which the praying person falls when praying in tongues. In Romans 8:26f. Paul speaks of the Spirit of God interceding for us with inexpressible sighs when we do not know how to pray. The words are incomprehensible to us, for secrets are spoken that leave the mind «blank». Yet there is no indication that we lose control of ourselves.

Quite the contrary – the person praying has not received the spirit of bondage (Rom. 8:15) and therefore retains his freedom. The fact that some prayers in charismatic communities seem unnatural or even alienating has more to do with the personal preferences of the person praying than with the Holy Spirit. It is not reprehensible to have one's own style, as long as it does not interfere with the proclamation of the Gospel (1 Cor. 14:23). We do not know what the apostle Paul's prayer was like in private, but in public he remained circumspect for the sake of the church (2 Cor. 5:13).

In this and other passages Paul speaks very clearly about the proper use of tongues in the church service. His reasons are also plausible (1 Cor. 14): Let us imagine that a non-believer walks into the church and finds the congregation praying in tongues out loud, then that person might very well believe that the people who are praying have gone mad. Unfortunately, I have experienced this. Visitors entered a church service for the first time and were under the impression that individual members of the congregation were suffering from a mental illness. Therefore, we cannot emphasize enough that speaking in tongues is not about individual performance, but about a higher purpose, which is to praise and thank God.

Much to my regret, the grievances I have just mentioned have caused many churches to throw the baby out with the bath water: Praying together in tongues has been banned from the church service altogether. But it is possible to be spiritual without becoming strange.

But let us return to the previously mentioned regulations for the various ways of dealing with tongues as we find them in the writings of the apostle Paul: As long as we practice praying in tongues for self-edification or in the form of corporate praise, it is not mandatory that there be an interpretation. However, when we speak in tongues to the congregation (1 Cor. 14:26), there must be a certain order (1 Cor. 14:28-31).

As far as personal edification is concerned, Paul wants everyone to speak in tongues if possible. But when it comes to contributing to the church service, the goal is to encourage people through clear, understandable teaching. Paul says therefore – as much as he appreciates personal prayer in tongues (14:19): I want to «… rather speak five words with my understanding, that I may teach others also, than ten thousand words in a tongue.» For the essential purpose of the service is not primarily personal edification, but the edification of the congregation.

SPEAKING IN TONGUES – AN INSIGNIFICANT GIFT?

At this point I would like to return to Paul's desire for everyone in
Corinth to speak in tongues (1 Cor. 14:5). The apostle clearly expresses that this gift is by no means insignificant or even the least of all,
as some people assume. Just because it is at the end of the list with
the interpretation of tongues does not mean that it is less important
than the other gifts. The order does not imply a ranking. Paul himself
prayed enthusiastically in tongues and highly valued this charism (1
Cor. 14:4f..15, 17f.; Rom. 8:26f.; Eph. 6:18). That is why he could very
boldly say of himself that he prayed more in tongues than anyone
else (1 Cor. 14:18). Although he did place value on the importance on
praying «with the mind», he still did not want to leave out the communication through the gift of the Spirit. He describes it as significant and desirable. Nevertheless, the fact that Paul narrows it down
so clearly in 1 Cor. 14 has more to do with the reason for the letter
than with the gift itself.[18]

HOW CAN THE GIFT OF TONGUES BE RECEIVED?

In my opinion, it would not be right to give precise instructions on how
to receive this desirable spiritual gift. Perhaps I would not succeed,
since the Holy Spirit works in His own way. Nevertheless, there are
some basic, helpful guidelines that may be familiar to some:
We have a promise from our Lord Himself that He will give us gifts
if we ask Him (Mt. 7:7). Paul in turn, advises us to seek the gifts
of the Spirit (1 Cor. 14:1). Thus, this gift is received through peti-
tion, persistent asking, and prayer with the laying on of hands. It
is certainly helpful to realize that what we are asking the Lord to
do is necessary and that it is good. Then, when God's Spirit gives

---

18 As mentioned earlier, the apostle only wrote about the gifts of the Spirit when he
was trying to correct grievances in the churches. The situation in Corinth must have
been disorderly. Apparently, brothers and sisters in that church believed that they
were required to preach and teach in tongues (1 Cor. 14:6, 19).

us words, we should also speak them. For some people it may be only fragments at first. But that doesn't matter, because every gift can start small and will develop as it is used. The important thing is that the recipient begins by saying the words out loud, but does not repeat them after anyone else.

As Christians living in Germany, who are used to order and sobriety, a new language may seem strange to us at first, because speaking in tongues is not understandable to the person praying (1 Cor. 14:14, 16). But the Holy Spirit, as we know, often breaks the mold in His work and likes to turn our structures upside down.

It is necessary to get involved in this foreign and heavenly realm. You are the one who activates this given gift. It is your decision of will. According to my understanding of the Scriptures, this is the only spiritual gift that we can practice whenever we want. In doing so, I believe each time anew that the gift of tongues is available to me. By using it in this way, my trust in the Lord grows, as does my faith that He will continue to bless me.

In 1 Corinthians 14:15, Paul declares, «I want to pray with the Spirit...». I believe we should do likewise and say to God, «I want to!»

10.2 The gift of prophecy

Of all the charisms of the Spirit, prophecy is mentioned most frequently in the New Testament. This fact suggests that prophecy was very common in the early church. There is also certainly a connection to the Jewish heritage of the communities. However, the encouraging prophecy of the New Testament clearly differs from the words of judgment of the prophets of ancient Israel. This tends to confirm our first assumption (that we encounter prophecy so naturally in the New Testament because it was part of the everyday life of the church at that time).

Literally translated the Greek word for prophecy (*profeteia*) means «to speak for someone else» or «to speak in place of someone else.» In Paul's list of spiritual gifts, the noun appears in the singular, which may indicate that each individual prophecy is a charism of God. Paul is not talking about the gift of being a prophet. According to the New Testament, sharing prophetic words is theoretically open to each of us, as long as the Holy Spirit empowers us to do so (Acts 2:17; 1 Cor. 14:24, 31). Paul directly invites all Christians to strive for this gift (1 Cor. 14:1, 39). Nevertheless, prophecies are given to believers with varying frequency and intensity.

The three levels of prophetic ministry

In the New Testament, there is explicit mention of prophets who form a separate group from those who minister with the spiritual gift of prophecy (1 Cor. 12:28f.; Acts 21:9f.): Not everyone who speaks prophetically in the New Testament is also a prophet. Paul makes a clear distinction here. I would hence like to speak of the gift of prophecy and the charismatic ministry or service of the prophet.

This difference is related to the varying degrees of empowerment of believers that I discussed at the beginning of this book. Prophecy, like all the gifts in the New Testament, is given more to one and less to another. A reference to this is also found in Rom. 12:6, where Paul mentions that prophecy, like the other gifts, is only found in a certain «measure». Again, we cannot assume that a human being possesses this gift, since it is the work of the Holy Spirit. Only in the case of speaking in tongues can a person himself take the initiative if he has received another language. And even there we see that it is used with varying intensity, as in the case of Paul, who spoke in tongues more than his brothers and sisters (1 Cor. 14:18). It is important to remember that the believer can also neglect the Lord's gifts, as happened to Timothy, and that these need to be re-ignited (1 Tim. 4:14; 2 Tim. 1:6). This is certainly a contributing factor to the fact that there are also differences in the expression of the gifts.

Some theologians, therefore, differentiate between different levels of prophecy. One division that I personally support is the three-level division as done by Mike Bickle and Michael Sullivant, for example. It is important to note, however, that this distinction can only be seen as a tool, for the Holy Spirit eludes our sharp demarcations, especially since there can be a constant development of the prophetic ministry.

LEVEL I – THE SIMPLE PROPHECY

Simple prophecy is basically for every Christian who reaches out to God. It does not contain exhortations, instructions, or predictions about the future. Of course, there are exceptions to the rule. The proportion of one's own thoughts and feelings that the prophesying person passes on is still quite high at this level (see figure on page 152). For this reason, congregations and churches tend to pay little attention to this form. We should nonetheless consider it as a distinct form of prophecy that can evolve. Depending on the context in which the believers are coming from, they will use different wording when they use this simple form: Some say that God spoke to them or that they received a word from God. Others receive a special revelation about the text as they read the Bible. Not all readers will probably agree with this view, but I believe that prophecy begins here. I would not discourage brothers and sisters who have received only one Bible verse from God for the church from sharing it. We should certainly not stop at this level, but ask for more revelations from God, because experience shows that if a person remains at this level for too long, the acceptance of the congregation decreases.

LEVEL II – THE GIFT OF PROPHECY

The second level concerns believers who regularly receive impressions, dreams, visions or other types of revelation. When I speak of this group of people, I like to call them "prophetically gifted" or "people with the gift of prophecy" (Rom. 12:6; 1 Cor. 12:10). This gift is distributed by the Spirit of God to those who earnestly ask our Lord for it (1 Cor. 14:24, 31). Messages that these people receive are usually very symbolic and appear in the form of parables and riddles. This group of people additionally receive prophetic information more often than the first group. People with prophetic gifts are well known in the congregation, are valued for their ministry, and are under the authority of the local church leadership.

A common misconception is that someone with the charism of prophecy necessarily has leadership responsibilities. However, this is not their duty, but the duty of local leaders who are gifted for it. The second level of prophecy is usually within the framework of encouragement, comfort, and exhortation (1 Cor. 14:3). People who minister responsibly in this gift also know that not everything they receive is from God - though the proportion of divine revelation may be greater at this level than at the first level (see Figure page 152).

How beneficial the effects of the gift of prophecy can be is illustrated by an incident I witnessed some time ago: A young man was given a word of comfort from the pulpit. In the conversation that followed, he told me that earlier that morning he had asked God for encouragement in a difficult matter. When he was then directly addressed in the service he learned that God had heard his prayer and that he would help him through this difficult time, his soul was lifted.

The office of prophet is held by believers whose ministry vaguely resembles that of the Old Testament prophets. I deliberately say "vaguely" because the ministry of the prophet in the Old Testament differs from that of the prophet in the New Testament.[19]

While the gift of prophecy is a gift of the Holy Spirit to individual believers, the ministry of the prophet is a gift of Jesus to the entire church for the equipping of believers (Eph. 4:11-14). Those who are called to this office often minister through signs and wonders, and the examination of their revelations always reveals that they accurately reflect the Word of God. However, this does not mean that they are infallible. Again: "Test everything and keep what is good." (1 Thess. 5:21). The credibility of these individuals is rarely in question, because they can already look back on many fulfilled prophecies and have thus confirmed their reliability.

Since their primary task is to equip and train the congregation, they require a great deal of patience and perseverance. Their ministry is extensive and involves a great deal of responsibility, which does not always make it easy.

A prophet's messages include not only words of encouragement, comfort, and exhortation, but also words of challenge. A prophet I know well was called one day to the bedside of a person who was on the verge of death. The relatives intensely prayed for healing and many of them were convinced that God would restore health. However, the Lord told the prophet that he had to prepare the family for the passing, because the goal of our life is eternity (1 Pet. 1:9) and man is destined to die (Heb. 9:27). Eventually, the person died in the sickbed. With this unpopular message, my friend drew much criticism.

---

19 *The Old Testament prophet stood between God and the people of Israel. The New Testament prophet is integrated into the church. While the Old Testament prophet claimed authority, the congregation should be able to recognize the New Testament prophet. He does not need to stand out because he does not have the same authority as the earlier prophet.*

He was called "unspiritual" and they even denied his faith. This experience was also painful for him. Nevertheless, both are part of the ministry of the prophet: To perform signs and wonders, but also to deliver messages that are not necessarily desired in earthly life. After all, his task is to proclaim God's word, not human speech.

I have met many people who move on levels I and II. In my opinion, the majority of Christians who speak prophetically in churches belong to one of these two groups. The ministry of the prophet is rarer, but exceedingly enriching to the Body of Christ. We will look at this ministry a little later.

THE WAY OF THE PROPHETIC WORD

Since I often minister prophetically and teach about it, I am always asked how God speaks through this gift. One phrase that I personally find quite appropriate is from Wayne Grudem. He writes about how prophecy first means "...speaking out human words to report something that God puts in our minds."[20] As stated earlier, not everything that man communicates in the context of prophecy is necessarily from God. My former companion Günther Karcher once said: "Prophecy is the reproduction of the thoughts of God, refracted through the prism of one's own language, and refracted through one's own personality."[21] Prophetic impressions, despite their divine origin, are therefore mixed with human impressions and need to be examined.

How do we now distinguish between impulses of the Holy Spirit and our own thoughts? To clarify this, I would like to refer to the story of creation. When God created Adam and Eve, the communication between Him and the two people was uninterrupted. They heard the voice of God (Gen. 3:8) and had a direct relationship with

---

20 Grudem: *Die Gabe der Prophetie*, 24.

21 Karcher: *Pneumatolgie II.*

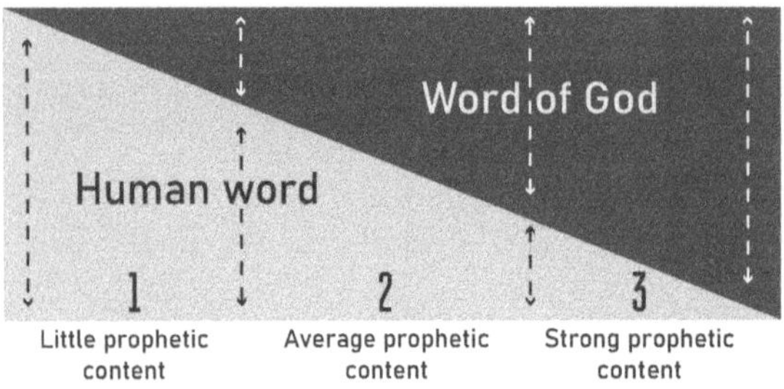

God. The fall of man, which we discussed in the first chapter of this book, interrupted this communication. Man was separated from God by sin. But God found a way to still get back in contact with him. In order to explain this, I must make a small excursion into the biblical doctrine of man.

The Bible conveys its own image of man or rather different images of man. It speaks of the spirit of man, of his soul, and his visible body. The spirit and the soul are often in contrast to the body, but in some places the two seem to be one and the same thing. Without going into detail, I would like to mention that the Bible does not know an abrupt separation of man into three different parts.

Therefore, I do not rigorously assume a tripartite conception of man. However, these three terms help me to better understand God's communication. Perhaps the following explanations will also help some readers.

The human spirit is considered to be born again once a person has become a child of God (Rom. 8:16). God speaks to this spirit through His Holy Spirit, who is able to have fellowship with the spirit of man (1 Cor. 2:10f.). Our spirit then passes on these impulses to our soul. The soul is considered to be the seat of a person's feelings, desires, and will. It is our "I", the center of our personality (Mt. 11:29; 26:38; Jn. 12:27). The body is the physical apparatus through which the spirit and soul connect with the material universe around us. Through the spirit, man also encounters God's words on other levels of existence.

In my opinion, all the works that God prepares happen three times: first with the Lord, then in the Spirit, and finally in the actual implementation. Moses also received the plan for the tabernacle on Mount Sinai before it could be put into practice and built (Ex. 25:1-9). In Mt. 6:10 it is not said for nothing: "Your kingdom come.

Your will be done on earth as it is in Heaven." And as we have already seen, Paul also speaks of the fact that the Lord has already prepared some things in heaven (Eph. 2:10).

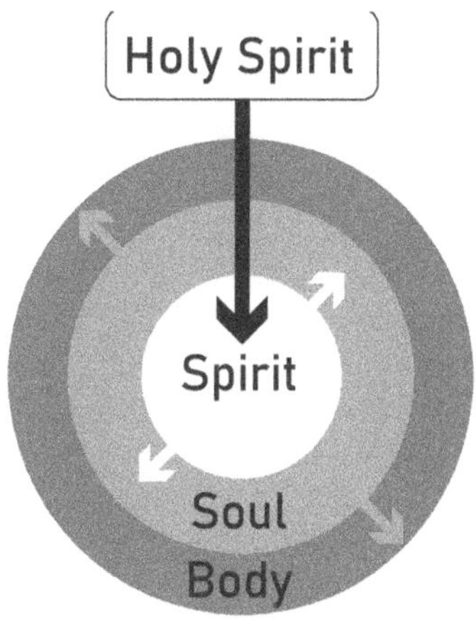

And now we will look at the importance of prophecy in this whole event: The prophetic word serves to show us what God intends to do. What is revealed can then be carried out. But not every prophecy is fulfilled, because man can also block its realization by his actions. God prepares things, but it does not always come to pass.

In theory, I was always aware that God had His own plans for my three sons. But in practice, it was not easy for me to think about it because I could not accept the paths they were taking. They were different than what I had imagined for my sons. As a result, I sang laments before the Lord. But there were times when my lamentations could no longer comfort me, and I was reminded of the Lord's Prayer. When I prayed for God's will to be done – on earth as it is in heaven, I realized something: I had no idea what this heavenly plan for them was. I didn't know what I was supposed to do as a father in order for God's will to take root in their lives. From then on, I changed how I prayed and asked the Lord what He was thinking and what He wanted. As it became more and more clear to me what God's plan for them was, I began to treat them differently. When we see people through God's eyes and treat them accordingly, we help them become what they are meant to be. When I did that, the frustration subsided, and with the grace of God, I began to prepare the heavenly things on earth. And it happened.

For a better classification, I would like to give a brief overview of the various ways in which God can speak to us. For when God speaks to people through the Holy Spirit, it is by no means always prophecy. The following table lists some of the most important other forms:

<table>
<tr><td colspan="1">GOD'S SPEAKING THROUGH THE SPIRIT</td></tr>
<tr><td>Revelation of one's own forsakenness (Acts 26:18)</td></tr>
<tr><td>Inspiration of the right words and thoughts in difficult situations (Mk. 13:11)</td></tr>
<tr><td>God's speaking through the Holy Scriptures (Jn. 14:26)</td></tr>
<tr><td>Insights into the invisible world (2 Ki. 6:16f.)</td></tr>
<tr><td>Visions (2 Cor. 12:2f.)</td></tr>
<tr><td>Different forms of prophecy</td></tr>
</table>

FORMS OF PROPHECY

What is true of His speaking through the Holy Spirit in general is also true of prophecy in particular: God does not always choose the same form to communicate with man. In the following, I would like to illustrate some important ways in which His prophecies reach people.

VISIONARY PROPHECY

Visionary prophecy is one of the most common forms of prophecy in our church congregations. The believers receive *images* inspired by the Holy Spirit and interpret them with the help of the same. An example of this is the animal vision of Peter, reported in Acts (Acts 10:9-24).

Dreams are another type of visionary prophecy. We see throughout the Bible that God speaks to people in their sleep through these experiences. Of course, not every dream we have is necessarily from God – all people dream in their sleep and this for different reasons. In Joel 3:1 we are promised that especially the elderly will receive dreams from God. In recent years, I have noticed an increase in the number of dreams given to me by the Spirit of God. Perhaps this is because I am getting older and because of my life experience I tend to pick apart the impressions I receive from the Lord more and more. Perhaps using dreams at night is God's way of bypassing some of my filters.

AUDITORY PROPHECY

But not everyone who is prophetically active receives figurative impressions from the Holy Spirit. God also speaks to people through *auditory prophecy*, revealing Himself in the words they hear within. To the person to whom the Holy Spirit speaks, the voice of God is audible, while it is not perceived by others around the receiver. A famous example of a person who experienced God's speaking in auditory form was Saul, who fell to the ground on the road to Damascus and heard Jesus' voice (Acts 9:3-19).

GLOSSAIC PROPHECY

The gift of tongues can also be a type of prophetic speaking in conjunction with the gift of interpretation, which is then called *glossaic prophecy*. For example, if someone in the congregation receives a message in tongues that is meant for the congregation, and another person is able to translate it by the Spirit into words that can be understood, then that message takes on a prophetic character. At present, we encounter this work of the Holy Spirit in German congregations less frequently than we did some 30 years ago. At that time it seemed to be the order of the day in many services. It is possible that this change is due to the fact that the form of the church services and the people who attend them have changed since then.

EXPRESSIVE PROPHECY

There is one type of prophecy that we find in the Bible that is almost no longer observed at the present time: It is *expressive prophecy*. It manifests itself in acts of signs. There are numerous examples of this in the Old Testament. Jeremiah, for example, performed many symbolic acts to visibly express God's words: These included hiding a belt of linen (13:1-11), demonstratively breaking a clay jar in front of his audience (19:1-13), and sinking a book in the Euphrates River (51:59-64). A New Testament example is the prophet Agabus, who bound his hands and feet with a belt to prophesy to Paul that he would be bound in the same way (Acts 21:10f.).

KERYGMATIC PROPHECY

A rather common form of prophecy, often not recognized as such, is *kerygmatic* prophecy (proclamation prophecy). In his time of preparation, the preacher seeks the presence of God and asks Him for the right thoughts and words for the proclamation.
He asks the Holy Spirit what is important to the congregation at that moment and allows Him to inspire him at the pulpit. Two biblical examples of this are the speeches of Peter (Acts 4:8) and of Stephen (Acts 7:55). It is said that both of them were full of the Holy Spirit while preaching. This kind of prophecy is especially effective because the listeners are usually open to the proclamation and the speaker also has a certain amount of time to make the message clear in various ways. In my opinion, every preacher should have the ambition that his sermon is Spirit-led.

REQUIREMENTS TO RECEIVE THE PROPHETIC GIFT

In order to hear God's voice, it is crucial to be a child of God, to follow Jesus with commitment and to place oneself in His service. Each person has received an individual call from God.[22] Some people may have the impression that God does not start thinking about them

---

22 *The term* calling *is used in different ways, and in the New Testament it is not always used as it is here. When I speak of calling, I mean a kind of plan or purpose of God for each individual person. It does not refer to the general way of salvation that the Lord has provided for all people, such as the sonship of God.*

until they come to faith, and then asks in surprise, "What am I going to do with him (or her) now? "

But it is not so! God's calling on an individual's life is part of His heavenly plan, which has been determined before the individual has ever lifted a finger for the Lord. Paul expresses this connection in Ephesians 2:10 as well:

For we are his workmanship, created in Christ Jesus for good works, which God prepared beforehand that we should walk in them.

It is important to engage in this calling. Neither Bible school nor discipline, fasting or prayer will change it. Spiritual exercises, however, can help to foster and release this divine predestination.

But it is not about getting God to appoint someone as a prophet or to give them a spiritual gift. Rather, it is to awaken the gifts and callings with which He has endowed us. Believers are to serve with the gift of grace they have been given (1 Pet. 4:10). Let us not forget: All gifts are important and valuable and have great significance for the Body of Christ. For the church to grow and develop in a healthy way, Jesus wants to use each of His children, so that we may serve one another with the gifts that have been given to us. Such an inner readiness is necessary to receive the charisms - including prophecy. It is written that we should be zealous for all gifts and especially for prophesy (1 Cor. 14:1; 2 Tim. 1:6; 1 Cor. 12:31). If we only pursue prophetic words, but disregard the other works that God has prepared, we may end up empty-handed.

But what does the right zeal for the prophetic, this striving or burning – as others translate it – look like in practice? For me personally, it means being in touch with Jesus and being in him, because without him we can do nothing (Jn. 15:1-8). He still speaks today and His sheep hear His voice (Jn. 10:27). But an essential key to recognizing the Shepherd is in our relationship with Him.

By zeal, then, we do not mean a cramped search. When people are obsessed with prophecy, there is a danger that they will end up focusing on the natural or the human and think that it is of the Spirit. Instead, they should turn to the Holy Spirit and His speaking, so that their focus is on Him – like a *(spiritual) antenna* that is set to receive. In all of this, it seems to me essential to keep one's own motives in mind.

We should ask ourselves why we seek this gift. Is it perhaps a small urge for recognition that lies dormant in our soul? Or is it perhaps a desire to achieve something special, to distinguish ourselves in this way?

These and similar motives are not good prerequisites for receiving God's gifts. The driving force of our striving should always be love; love for God, for the church, and for people.

OBSTACLES TO HEARING THE VOICE OF GOD

Even if we meet all the necessary requirements to receive the prophetic gift, this does not necessarily mean that we are able to hear God's voice. There are some factors that can make it difficult or prevent it altogether. I would like to briefly outline them below:

Lack of the Word of God The Word of God makes us sensitive to the voice of God (Col. 3:16).
Lack of close relationship with God The deeper and more intense the relationship, the more sensitive our hearing becomes (Heb. 4:14).
Lack of knowledge of God's grace When our image of God is distorted, we find it difficult to perceive His voice (1 Cor. 4:1-2).

> **Lack of faith**
> Lack of faith limits one's willingness to hear, and faith is desired
> by the Lord (Heb. 11:6).

> **Lack of obedience**
> Disobedience blocks God's voice and the gap between what we say
> and what we do harms us (King Saul in 1 Sam.).

THE PURPOSE OF PROPHECY

Everything the Lord does has a meaning. Nothing happens in vain, and so prophecy should also serve its purpose. First of all, there is pastoral counseling. Prophecy always has this purpose, otherwise it is questionable, because it does not meet the requirements of the Holy Scripture. In 1 Cor. 14:3f. we find this triumvirate of the prophetic mission, expressing the above pastoral emphasis: edification, exhortation and consolation.

But he who prophesies speaks to men for edification and exhortation and consolation. He who speaks in one language edifies himself; but he who prophesies edifies the church.

In addition, prophecy can serve to free people for their calling and to accompany and strengthen the gospel message as a sign. We will learn more about this in the next sections.

In general, it should be noted that prophecy is not primarily concerned with the future. Although this may be a common assumption, it is not true. Prophecy speaks about all times: past, present, (Acts 5:1) and future (Acts 11:28). Its purpose is not to foretell what is to come – like a kind of Christian divination, but to edify, encourage, and comfort.

In the following we will consider these three fundamental aspects of the pastoral mission of prophecy:

PROPHECY FOR EDIFICATION

The term edification comes from the building industry. A building is created according to the methods and plan of an architect. The architect thought through the project and made sure that it is now a solid and load bearing structure. In the same way, prophecy also builds up its recipients and gives them stability. However, this does not mean that prophecy must always be pleasant (in the sense of "edifying"). Edification can also take place where a person is lovingly corrected.

EXHORTATION PROPHECY

Exhortation is called *paraklesis* in the New Testament. Unfortunately, there are still some misconceptions about exhortation. The term has little in common with the meaning as it is used in German. Here an exhortation is first a reproof for wrongdoing. Unfortunately, some still think that the term in 1 Corinthians 14:3 is to be understood in the same way.
I have even heard of prophecies that have been in the nature of a warning. But *paraklesis* also means to encourage and to assist. So it is not an admonition or a rebuke as we are used to in modern language, but to point a person in the right direction. The person needs guidance and support on his journey. Time and again, he gets off track or loses direction. Prophecy provides help and guidance so that we can reach our destination.

PROPHECY FOR COMFORT

Finally, prophecy is also balm for the heart. Consolation[23] lifts up a person in his suffering and despondency. Each of us knows how often

---

23 *The Greek word paramythia means «to speak kindly to, to cheer up» and is unique in the New Testament. In the ancient papyri, it means «consolation» after a troubling or distressing situation.*

such encouragement can make a decisive difference. We are often helpless in the face of sickness, loss, and other problems. That is why our Lord gave us prophecy: To reveal His thoughts about us and to comfort us.

In each of these cases it has become clear: The real purpose of prophecy is to provide solutions and to offer help. Prophecy does not leave people standing in the rain, but always offers hope, a new perspective and a way out.

PROPHECY FOR THE RELEASE OF CALLING

As already indicated, the usefulness of prophecy is not limited to the pastoral dimension. It also reveals spiritual gifts and the potential that dwells within us (1 Tim. 1:18). The Creator not only knows our actual state, but also what we can become. Through prophecy, we see ourselves with the eyes of the heart of God. Galileo Galilei once wrote, "You cannot teach a man anything; you can only help him to find it within himself."

Prophecy shows us the way so that we can discover what God has placed within us.

Day in and day out I see people who are not living up to their God-given potential. If it were up to me, I would like to clearly express my opinion to them. My words would probably be more of an admonition in the German sense. But that is not the way our Lord speaks to His children. When I remember that prophecy is given to serve people in a threefold pastoral counseling way, it helps me to meet them appropriately.

PROPHECY TO SUPPORT THE MESSAGE OF THE GOSPEL

Now let us mention one last important use of prophecy, which is its evangelistic character that Paul emphasizes in 1 Corinthians 14:24.

But if all prophesy, and an unbeliever or outsider enters, he is convicted by all, he is called to account by all.

Part 3: Serving in the grace of God | **161**

It becomes clear that prophecy develops a tremendous effectiveness when it comes to God's correction of unbelievers and making Himself known. A New Testament example of how this work of the Holy Spirit unfolds in a person's life is the woman at Jacob's well (Jn. 4:16-19).

I, too, have seen it happen a number of times that strangers have come to a service and have been spoken to by the Holy Spirit through a prophecy. Suddenly they realized that there is a God who knows them very well, who is seriously interested in them and who wants to help them. Because of this, they decided to engage with God and get to know Him.

The power that can come from a single prophecy is beyond anything man can do. One day, one of our youth leaders came to me and excitedly reported that a new teenager had decided to follow Jesus after I had ministered to him prophetically. This was the first time this young man had attended the meeting because a friend had invited him.

He didn't really know what to do with the church, but he wanted to claim prophetic prayer for himself. After I prayed for him, he felt a longing to be part of the church and to learn more about Jesus. He understood that he had a Father in heaven and was very touched by this. My youth leader said to me in amazement, "We haven't even managed to tell him about Jesus yet and he is already a believer." There was nothing more I could tell him about it except that these things are the result of the Holy Spirit's speaking to people. Prophecy brings the reality of God into the lives of people who do not yet know Him.

COMMUNICATING THE PROPHECY

Let us now come to a very important aspect which concerns above all the bearers of the divine messages: For not only the "what" or the "what for" is crucial, but especially the "how"! If a prophecy is not accepted, this does not necessarily mean that it was not inspired by the Holy Spirit. The reason for the rejection may also be due to the way the message was delivered. Some people lack awareness of how they affect others. We may pay special attention to what we say, but we forget that there are other parts of us that speak volumes. The individual components of communication have a different impact. According to Albert Mehrabian[24] the content has an effect of about 7%. The manner of speaking has a much greater influence, namely 38%. The body language, which makes up the highest part of all with 55%, is often underestimated. The remaining components are formed by other factors such as environment and time of the sharing. Mehrabian's thesis is called a myth by many of his guild. Whether or not it may be true: We can see that the other components of a message can easily be underestimated.

Even if these factors cannot be weighted in such a way, the pure content of a message is never the only thing that counts. We must be aware of these connections when we pass on prophecies! Besides, people are different and understand messages in different ways. Consequently, we should keep in mind the words of the famous behavioral scientist Konrad Lorenz:

Thought is not yet said, said is not yet heard, heard is not yet understood, understood is not yet agreed, agreed is not yet applied and applied is not yet retained.

Sharing the prophetic impression is not only about delivering a message, but also about considering the people involved. Prophecy is not meant to set others straight, but to help them. A negative example from the Old Testament is the prophet Jonah. He expected that the prophecy of judgment would to be fulfilled - regardless of the losses. When the people repented and God spared them, Jonah became angry (Jonah 3:10; 4:1-4). Jonah had not understood what God was about. We have seen in 1 Cor. 12 that the effects of the Spirit are mentioned. In chapter 13, however, it is shown that they

------

24 *Mehrabian: The Journal of Counselling Psychology, 248-252.*

have value only when given in love. It is not until chapter 14 that we finally learn how and where the gifts are to be used. This sequence is not accidental, but Paul's intention is to describe love as the basis of the gifts.

Despite the supernatural nature of God's revelations, it is important to note that we always receive them in full control of our consciousness. In the Greek environment of the New Testament, a distinction was made between mantic and prophecy. Mantic means divination in a kind of trance and under external control. The person speaking is only a medium, not a consciously acting subject. In New Testament prophecy, on the other hand, the message is delivered while the person is awake and clearly conscious.

Thus, Paul clearly states in 1 Cor. 14:32 that "...the spirits of the prophets are subject to the prophets." However, this does not mean that the *Holy Spirit* is subordinate to the prophet, but rather that the own spirit of the prophet is subordinate to him. Again, let us remember that we have not received a spirit "...that makes us slaves..." (Rom. 8:15). The servant of God always remains in control when prophesying and does not need to speak prophetically under irresistible compulsion. Therefore, it is inappropriate to make a spiritual spectacle. Passing on the prophetic words can be quite natural. Some people also, out of ignorance, change their voice during the communication of prophecy and adopt a threatening attitude. Again, this is not commanded.

Furthermore, in terms of timing, we may know that the Holy Spirit is not tied to a church service. The prophesier can therefore determine the right time for himself – and he should, because there are situations that are appropriate for receiving a prophecy, but not for speaking it.

The following phrases, as they are commonly used, may be helpful as an introduction:
-    "I have the impression that the Lord wants to tell us ..."
-    "The Lord has spoken to me ..."
-    "I have seen a picture ..."

In sharing, however, it is not the outward form that is essential, but what God has spoken. For the benefit of the individual listener or the congregation, the messenger should be brief when prophesying. There is no need for a long speech or explanation of what he has received, unless it is a kerygmatic prophecy and the local church leadership has given the green light. We should only share what we have received from the Lord, and not add anything to it (Prov. 30:6).

In all of this, it is important to submit to the local spiritual leaders. The one who prophesies is not the only one led by the Spirit. The local leaders also know when the time is right to deliver the message. The bottom line is that the Holy Spirit works in many ways in the church, not just through individuals. There should be a certain spiritual order so that everyone can be blessed (1 Cor. 14:29-33). For example, if too many impressions and effects of the Spirit are strung together, they may overwhelm the listeners. The service simply becomes too long, and at some point it is no longer possible to take proper note of what is being said. In such situations, it may not be advisable to pass on the Spirit's words immediately, since they are meant to be heard.

The decision as to how to deal with the word that is spoken is always left up to the person in question. Even the prophet Agabus only told Paul what to expect in Jerusalem. He had carried out his mission. What was to happen next was left to Paul, and he did not try to persuade him to act (Acts 21:10-12).

TESTING PROPHECY

Paul teaches us not to despise prophecy, but to test it as well (1 Cor. 14:29; 1 Thess. 5:20f.). Prophetic words have edified and blessed many people and congregations, but on the other hand have also caused many conflicts and hardships. The causes of such negative effects can vary. In some cases, there has certainly been a mishandling of the prophecies; in others, there has simply been the work of false prophets. Both Jesus (Mt. 7:15; 24:11, 24) and the apostles (e.g. 1 Jn. 4:1) have warned against the latter. It is all the more important to look first at the prophesier himself.

People who spread false prophecies often gain considerable followings, while others who proclaim the messages of the Holy Spirit are sometimes even ostracized for their ministry.

A person's acceptance or disapproval from his environment is therefore not necessarily revealing. Jeremiah 23:11-26 describes false prophets. They are people who tolerate sin in themselves and others, are dishonest, and say things that others want to hear. In Col. 2:18 Paul also warns against people who are selfish and vain. Those who are not willing to submit to local leadership or to have the prophecies tested have no right to speak in the name of God. As a matter of principle, we should not listen to people who make themselves great instead of our Lord. Also, seditious personalities who gather people around them in order to follow a particular path in theology should not find an audience, for our God is a God of peace (1 Cor. 14:33). Furthermore, there is a difference between prophecy and teaching - but more about that later. Most of the time, such personalities do not produce good "fruit" and so we can expose them (Mt. 7:20).

But even if the person from whom the prophetic words come is not questionable but godly, we have no guarantee that God is speaking through him. As I have explained, prophecy always contains human elements, and as humans we are fallible. We see in the New Testament that prophets prophesied. However, the church should assess their words (1 Cor. 14:29). It is helpful not only to examine the prophecies on our own, but also to seek the opinions of more mature brothers and sisters. Their experience and spiritual intuition may reveal things that we may have missed. Christians therefore need the ability to discern right from wrong. In the following, I would like to offer some test criteria for this.

1. It glorifies Jesus

Let us note that prophecy always glorifies Jesus first and foremost. He has priority above all else (Col. 1:18) and should always be the center of what is said. Any words that glorify people and other things do not originate from the Holy Spirit. A prophetic word must also never be an occasion for pride. This applies to both those prophesying and those listening. It is the work of the Holy Spirit and is not an award for some special religious accomplishment.

2. It does not replace Scripture

Prophecy is different from teaching. While in the Bible normative, theological and ethical guidelines are given to us by the authors, the prophetic word is a spontaneous impulse of the Holy Spirit. It cannot replace the written Word of God and should in no way contradict its witness. If the content of a prophecy causes me to act in a way that is contrary to the biblical message, then it is probably more a matter of human thought than an impulse from the Holy Spirit. The prophesier should always submit to the inspired Holy Scriptures. The writings of the eyewitnesses of Jesus formed the canon of the New Testament, while the individual writings found a general acceptance among the early witnesses of Jesus. As a result, it was completed at the Synod of Rome (382). It will not be changed again to add new special doctrines and exceptions.

This may be clear to most of us, but unfortunately there are still churches in which prophetic words are passed on that are far removed from the testimony of the Bible. Although they obviously contradict Scripture, they are believed and acted upon. This must not be!

I was once approached by a man who thought he had heard from the Lord that he should leave his wife for a younger woman. I asked him if he really believed that God would change his mind about marriage because of him.

Another Christian told me that God had revealed to him that a division in the church was imminent and that preparation was necessary. In such a case, there is a serious question in my mind as to what is the name of the lord from whom these people are receiving such messages.

3. It fulfills the threefold purpose

Edification, exhortation, and consolation form the main purpose of prophecy (1 Cor. 14:3-4). Prophetic words that do not contain this triad should not be immediately dismissed. However, I think it makes sense to take a closer look at them. If a prophecy is devastating or discouraging, then the message or the messenger should be questioned.

4. It brings about freedom and not dictatorship

Prophecy inspired by the Holy Spirit brings about freedom, not bondage (2 Cor. 3:17). It is never designed to establish a spiritual dictatorship. Everything that destroys the independence, individuality, and responsibility is not of the Holy Spirit. God did not create us to be puppets, but gave each of us our own personality. The peace of the Holy Spirit should be present with us and reign in our hearts (Col. 3:15).

5. It comes true

Of course, a prophecy should also come true if it is truly inspired by God. Especially in the Old Testament, we see clearly that this criterion was important (Deut. 18:21f.). The examination of a prophecy on the basis of the fact of whether it is actually fulfilled or not must, however, be done with reservations: It does not apply to all prophecies, since we ourselves can contribute to prophecies not being fulfilled.

The Lord may make promises to a person, but if the person does not act on them, those promises will not be fulfilled. The people of Israel were also told that they would enter the Promised Land, but through their actions they were ultimately forced to spend 40 years in the desert (Deut. 32:13). Therefore, timelines should be considered with caution when we receive prophecies, and it is not advisable to pass them on.

6. It flows from a purified source

Finally, the way of life of the person who is prophesying should be examined. Even if it is not a false prophet (as described above), the life of the messenger may allow some conclusions to be drawn: There may be issues that are on his mind at the moment and therefore become supposedly prophetic words, etc.

AREAS WHERE PROPHECY IS NOT ADVISABLE

False prophecies carry a great risk of misuse and they have caused massive damage in the past. Therefore, I would like to conclude by pointing out some areas where prophecy should not be used.

One sensitive area of life is the subject of matchmaking. I have met people who have entered into a relationship and eventually marriage because of a prophecy. Afterwards, the people involved were disappointed in God. No one should base his or her choice of partner solely on the testimony of one or more people. There are other important criteria for choosing a partner. Furthermore, people tend to declare their own desires as the will of God when they desire something particularly. Therefore, both partners (not just one!) must have received a word from the Lord before making such an important decision.

Once a man came up to me and said that he had a bone to pick with God. He had given him an extremely difficult wife who did not suit him at all. Their marriage was a disaster. What contribution he himself had made to his misery, I do not know. So I lovingly told him that he had not been given his head just to wear hats. He could have used it back then.

Major life decisions should never be made on the basis of prophecy alone. The Lord often reveals through an inspired word what is living in the person and does not show completely different ways. The prophetic word is not, therefore, a means of determining careers or vocations. These decisions are made by the individual in a process of prayer and identification with God Himself. In order to avoid mistakes and to set a good course in the important questions of life, it is therefore important to have good counselors in addition to the spiritual gifts of "word of wisdom" and "word of knowledge". We should also be on guard when prophecy is used for the purpose of placing people in positions of authority in the church or for the purpose of removing people from certain positions. I have seen many instances where positions in churches have been filled very poorly because of a supposed instruction from God, which has only led to tension and conflict. Sometimes prophetic words have been misused to get rid of certain people who were thought to be wrong in their positions. Out of fear of confrontation, prophecy was then used as an excuse. However, this is not the right way to handle these matters. The leadership of the Church is called to take a stand here. Unfortunately, it is not uncommon for prophecy to be used in a similarly manipulative way to impose certain tastes and styles on the brothers and sisters in the congregation. It must not be used for this purpose either.

As Christians who have the gift of prophecy, we should also be careful with business decisions and donations. Sadly, I have seen people give large sums of money to churches based on certain prophecies. They were promised that they would receive special financial blessings if they would obey the Lord's request and make a substantial donation. However, I believe that giving should always be done voluntarily and without any outside influence (Acts 5:4; 2 Cor. 9:7).

11 THE FIVEFOLD MINISTRY

Whoever speaks of enabling grace and the gifts of grace (charismata) cannot ignore a significant passage in the New Testament: In Ephesians 4:11ff. the apostle Paul lists the five charismatic ministries that Jesus gave to His church:

And he gave the apostles, the prophets, the evangelists, the shepherds and teachers, to equip the saints for the work of ministry, for building up the body of Christ, until we all attain to the unity of the faith and of the knowledge of the Son of God, to mature manhood, to the measure of the stature of the fullness of Christ, so that we may no longer be children, tossed to and fro by the waves and carried about by every wind of doctrine, by human cunning, by craftiness in deceitful schemes. Rather, speaking the truth in love, we are to grow up in every way into him who is the head, into Christ. (Eph. 4:11-15)

The groups of people mentioned here are called "charismatic ministries" by some and "ministry gifts" by others. Both names, I believe, are legitimate and consistent with the New Testament witness. It is true that we do not encounter the terms just mentioned, not even the term "fivefold ministry" that I have used, but we are given a set of five ministries. It is clear from the text that these special gifts are not given to all believers. It is also clear that they are all focused on preaching, teaching, and leading. In fact, it seems as if Paul could take for granted that the ministries were known. The list shows clear differences from the other gifts I have described in recent chapters: These are not gifts (*charismata*) that the Spirit works or places in His service, but ministries that Christ Himself institutes as head of His body. In this passage we are furthermore not talking about the effects of the Spirit, but about *people* flesh and blood, who – empowered by their
Lord – perform important functions in the church of Jesus Christ. *They are themselves* gifts of God, distributed not for the blessing of

individuals but for the blessing of the congregation. In this regard, it seems to me that the term "ministry" is appropriate, although it should not give the impression that the concept of succession of offices exists in the Bible.

11.1 THE MEANING OF THE FIVEFOLD MINISTRY

Jesus Himself ordains certain people for one of these special ministries. We see this approach frequently in Scripture. God calls people and enables them to do His work. This is what we are told in the Old Testament, for example, with regard to the prophets. In the New Testament as well, we can see how the Lord chooses people for a particular task. One of the outstanding examples is certainly Saul of Tarsus himself. In the selection of those who are called, however, it is neither a special education nor an extraordinary professional career that counts, but God's grace alone.

But for what purpose does God appoint these groups of people? Paul describes several goals that God wants to accomplish through the ministry of these people. The primary purpose of the ministries is the growth of the church in Christ (Eph. 4:15): At the beginning of the letter to the Ephesians (Eph. 1:18-23), Paul prays that the Ephesians might recognize the riches to which they have been called. The crucified and resurrected Christ has ascended into heaven and has taken His place at the right hand of the Father. He rules from heaven over all powers. He is the head of the Church, which is His body on earth. The calling of His followers is to grow toward the exalted Christ and invade His realm. This is done by His body reaching the whole creation with the Gospel. Specifically, this requires that the ministries build up the church with their gifts (Eph. 4:12).

They are responsible for equipping the saints for ministry. Through the ministries, the brothers and sisters are equipped with everything they need to help build the work of Jesus Christ. In other words, they are trained, advised, and accompanied by apostles, prophets, evangelists, shepherds, and teachers, so that they can develop into mature followers of Christ and serve according to their measure of grace.

It is always relieving for me as a pastor to keep this image of the body of Christ in mind that Paul describes here in Ephesians: A church in which individuals work together in their full strength and maturity. In our society, the opposite tendency is emerging: It is becoming more and more of a service society, as many traditional professions are disappearing due to technological advances. Unfortunately, this has also led to the congregation often being seen as a service provider for religious services. This development also affects the expectations of leaders: Pastors and ministers must handle all kinds of administrative and operational tasks as part of their employment. This leaves less and less time for the spiritual ministry for which they were called. And even there, the demands on them are great.

The apostles in the early Jerusalem congregation were maneuvered into a similar situation. They realized that this "was not good" (Acts 6:2) and looked around for Spirit-filled people who would take care of the organizational and charitable work.

It should give us pause when called leaders are unable to carry out their ministry because they are involved in other activities that are tied to an employment relationship. In a church built according to God's plan, leaders must have the freedom they need to equip the saints. The whole church will ultimately benefit. The body of Christ cannot thrive if the brothers and sisters in the charismatic ministries are doing work that others are called to do. It grows when the apostles, prophets, evangelists, shepherds, and teachers are able to equip and release the other believers for ministry.

LEVELS OF GROWTH

In some circles, the five-fold ministry is also referred to figuratively as "the strong hand of God" – as in Jens Kaldewey's book of the same name, which deals with these ministries. The idea behind this designation is that each of these ministries is like a finger of the hand that performs a specific function. All five have their special place and although each of them is a finger, they are each given a different significance. Together they make up the whole hand. It is important that we as a church keep all the "limbs" within a certain radius, for a hand is limited if all the fingers are not present.

The five-fold ministry makes the church flourish in various areas of congregational life. The ministries also work together in such a way that the church ideally thrives equally in all of these areas. In the current church landscape, we encounter mostly shepherds, teachers, and evangelists, with the latter being rather rare in relation to the other two. This is very unfortunate, because any one-sidedness will sooner or later lead to deficiencies and extremes. When an apostle is released into ministry, he usually helps to open up new areas through his pioneering and founding ministry. The prophet, on the other hand, speaks the thoughts and directives of God over the Body of Christ and over individuals so that they may be guided appropriately. The evangelist makes sure that people encounter the gospel and come to know the Lord. In this way, he provides the basis for the quantitative growth of the congregation. The shepherd cares for the individual. Through his care and the space he creates, the body grows together.

The teacher opens the depths of the Scriptures to a congregation and builds them up in the knowledge of God. The following chart outlines these five areas of growth:

MINISTRY	AREAS OF GROWTH
Apostle	Proliferation
Prophet	Relationship with God
Evangelist	Quantity
Shepherd	Love for one another
Teacher	Knowledge of God

Before we now take a closer look at the individual offices, I would like to point out that the exact number of offices is a matter of dispute. There is a small formal detail that suggests that the canon of ministries described here is not a fivefold canon, but rather a fourfold ministry: It is the missing article between the last two designations in the row of the fivefold series. From a purely grammatical point of view, the shepherds and the teachers should form the same group.[25] Some emphasize that this statement is also precise, since every shepherd must necessarily be able to teach (1 Tim. 3:2; 2 Tim. 2:24). In my opinion, the office of the shepherds is, in fact, closely related to the office of the teachers. Therefore, the two together form their own group within the fivefold ministry. This connection is evident in Paul's letters. It is probable that the terms describe overlapping functions (cf. 1 Cor. 12:28-29 and Gal. 6:6), but are not identical, so my basic assumption is a separate teaching ministry. This is also mentioned separately at an earlier point (Acts 13:1). Apostles and prophets enter a similar covenant with each other as well (Eph. 2:20; 3:5). Accordingly, the ministries can also be divided into three subgroups. In the following considerations it will become clear in what way they are related to each other.

It also seems worth noting that probably none of the ministries can be found in pure form. Paul was described not only as an apostle, but also as a teacher (Acts 13:1). The gift profile of each person is distinctly unique and so are the ministries.

11.2 APOSTLE

The apostle and the prophet are mentioned first by Paul. This is certainly not done without reason, for in other places it is clear that these offices are fundamental to the church (Eph. 2:20; 1 Cor. 12:28; Rev. 21:14). Together with our Lord as the cornerstone, they have a supporting role for the body of Christ.

---

25 *In Greek, when two words are joined by only one article, it indicates a close association of the two terms. So, strictly speaking, there are four points in the list.*

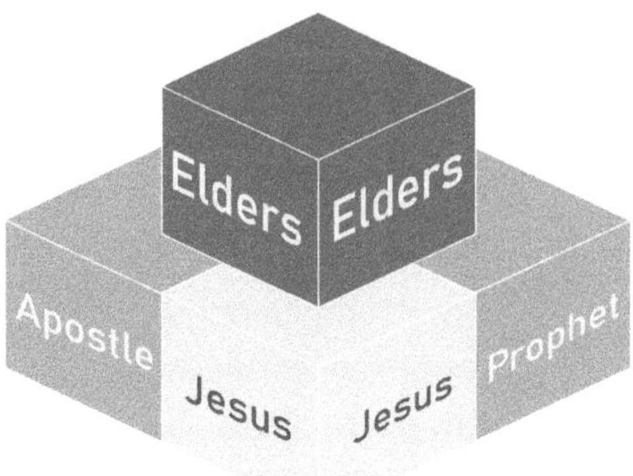

The term apostle (apostolos) actually refers to a messenger or commissioner with a very special role: It is a person who is sent out with a message. It is remarkable in this context that according to the ancient Semitic law of messengers, the messenger himself was considered the sender.

By virtue of his role as a messenger, he had the right and obligation to make decisions for the employer, but only for the duration of the mission. The New Testament apostles were commissioned and sent by Christ Himself (1 Cor. 12:5).

The New Testament testimony tells us of various authorized messengers of God. First, we usually think of the twelve apostles or disciples from Jesus' immediate circle, then the other well-known and influential figures of the New Testament – especially Paul. However, there must have been a multitude of apostles who did not appear in the New Testament. Even the Son of God is called an apostle by the writer of Hebrews (Heb. 3:11), but this designation for Jesus is unique in the New Testament. This is understandable, however, because He was also sent by the Father (Jn. 17:18).

The apostle can also be seen as a kind of team leader for the other ministries. We see in the New Testament that the apostles appointed local leaders, licensed certain brothers and sisters to teach, and sent others out (Acts 14:23; 15:24; Tit. 1:5). Not everyone could call themselves an apostle. Their ministry was accompanied by manifestations of the supernatural dimension of the Kingdom of God in the form of signs and wonders (Acts 4:33; 8:4-7; Rom. 15:19; 2 Cor. 12:12). The work as a church planter and pioneer was also seen as a confirmation of the apostolic office (1 Cor. 9:2). However, people who falsely claimed to be apostles were severely criticized (2 Cor. 11:13; Rev. 2:2).

The apostle is considered the master builder of the church (1 Cor. 3:10). He lays the foundations and promotes growth. Individual leaders as well as entire congregations are advised, stabilized, and equipped by him. His primary goal, however, is not the cultivation of a single church, but rather the extension of the heavenly kingdom on earth (Rom. 15:20; 2 Cor. 10:16). His perspective is therefore a kingdom perspective.

An apostle can also be called a missionary strategist. As a pioneer, he starts and develops new things. He finds and promotes young leaders. He creates plans and concepts so that the vision of God can be realized. He is also the one who constantly works to see that they are carried out. Where the apostle enters the scene, something must be set in motion because he is advancing the cause of Jesus Christ. He thinks and works on a different scale of magnitude than the local leaders. While others focus on the local, he focuses on the national and international. He is able to spot current developments and seeks God's strategies and plans to respond to new challenges. His character is characterized by creativity, flexibility and resilience. He has great patience with others and is not controlling. Where the apostolic ministry takes hold, free spaces are created. It is a gift for times of awakening and change. In the present, when life is becoming more complex and upheavals are occurring at breakneck speed, apostolic leaders are especially important.

Where there are no apostles, an essential member of the body is missing. This fact is made painfully clear to local congregations time and again. I have often observed what happens when apostles leave their place in a congregation or region to serve elsewhere. The churches suffered a bitter loss. They desperately try to fill the void in various ways. New people were positioned and attempts were made to integrate various concepts that would give the Fellowship a new lease on life. It was denied that the past momentum was attributable to one person. After all, the body does not depend on people, but on the head of the church, which is Christ. But all the good arguments, structural changes, and concepts could not replace the missing apostle.

Certainly, the local church is dependent on its divine head, but this head has decided to build His church on the foundation of the apostles and prophets (Eph. 2:20; 1 Cor. 12:28). His means are people.

Of course, the apostle does not have all the gifts at his disposal, and his ministry involves circumstances that may not be to the liking of everyone in the local church: He works first on the church and not in the church. His focus is outward and less inward. Since his ministry is primarily intercongregational, he cannot be in one place on a regular basis and thus has a greater distance from the brothers and sisters in the congregation. It is also unlikely that pastoral care will be part of his area of competence. A congregation, which keeps an eye on the charisms of its members and promotes those, can cope well with this fact. After all, the Lord has also given the gift of mercy and appointed people as shepherds.

11.3 PROPHETS

Anyone who wants to talk about the office of the prophet cannot avoid looking at the prophets of the Old Testament. They were God's mouthpieces in the past. But obviously the office of the New Testament prophet is different from that of the Old Testament prophet. The latter seem to have had much more responsibility. They were to see that the people of Israel kept God's commandments Much was expected of them, and they had to endure severe hardships, like Hosea or Jeremiah. But with Jesus' death on the cross, the reception of the Holy Spirit, and Pentecost, these specific tasks of the prophets were transferred to a large part of Christianity. God used to reveal Himself to a small group of prophets to speak to His people. Now He is speaking to a much larger group (1 Cor. 2:9f.). John the Baptist was probably the last Old Covenant prophet we encounter in the Bible. After him, a new age began.

Therefore, the prophetic office did not disappear from the world at that time, but it has been changed since then. The prophets of the Old Testament were to expose the frivolous attitude of the people toward the law, to call them to repentance, to expose false messages, and finally to encourage the people. Through the profound change wrought by Jesus' incarnation, death, and resurrection, this level of work is not required of the New Testament prophet in the same way. What remains is the nature of the calling and appointment as a prophet. Nowhere in the New Testament does it appear that prophets were called into office by men. God continues to commission the prophets Himself. Besides John the Baptist and Jesus, who calls himself a prophet (Lk. 4:24), the New Testament knows of numerous other prophets. In some churches they seem to have formed their own group (1 Cor. 14:29). Examples include Agabus, Jude, and Silas (Acts 11:28; 15:32).

A few paragraphs earlier I pointed out that the New Testament distinguishes between the gift of prophecy and the office of prophet. The gift is theoretically available to everyone – but in different forms, as we have already seen. The office of prophet, however, is tied to one person (Eph. 4:11). That person is appointed by God.

A prophet seeks God in order to receive revelations and visions from Him. Like the Old Testament prophets – he can also be called God's mouthpiece (Jer. 15:19), because he communicates the present will of God for the church (Rev. 19:10). He foretells future events (Acts 11:28; Rev. 22:6f.), receives the heartbeat of God for the church and the individual. Therefore, a prophet is also a person who seeks to be close to God (Jn. 13:23). The revelations he receives are a blessing to the church in many ways. Through him the Lord gives:

- Divine renewal
- Divine instruction
- Divine warning
- Divine exhortation

- Divine help and comfort
- Divine encounters

Through a prophet, the horizons of God are opened to others. It is through him that the individual believer is led to take his or her place in the church (Acts 13:1-3). He kindles the gifts of the Spirit in them (1 Tim. 4:14). He also helps the church to know its condition and the purposes of God. This creates a new dynamic and brings it to maturity (Eph. 4:13).

Prophets emphasize the importance of devotion and sanctification. They place a high value on the holiness of God and the will of God to be valued and respected.

Agabus' prophecy about the coming famine under the emperor Claudius (Acts 11:28) also shows that prophets are relevant to society outside the church.

Prophets are usually spontaneous personalities who do well with change. Their ministry is not tied to a local church, as can be seen, for example, in the person of John (Rev. 2:1-3,22). Yet they are established in a church setting, recognized and embedded in a church landscape – not "freelance artists" who are unwilling to be accountable to anyone. Some time ago, a prophet wanted to invite himself to our church. I asked him to whom he submitted and where his spiritual leaders were. He replied that he did not answer to anyone because he served the worldwide body of Christ. I then recommended to him that he knock on the door of the global church. He certainly belongs to the worldwide body of Jesus – as do all Christians. But it is only through the sum of the local churches that the global church takes shape.

Prophets, along with apostles, lay the foundation of the church (Eph. 2:20). If the office of the prophet is not filled, then not only is the church missing an important organ of equipping, but it is also wandering blindly – in ignorance of God's purposes.

In a similar way to the apostle, the distance of the prophet from the people can be a problem for some brothers and sisters – especially if he or she has a leadership role in a local church. Because of their nonregional ministry, they are not always found locally.

11.4 EVANGELISTS

The term "evangelist" (*euangelistes*) actually rarely appears in the New Testament. It is used only twice outside of the list of offices in Ephesians 4:11 (Acts 21:8; 2 Tim. 4:5). The word describes a person who *proclaims* good news. It is obvious what is meant by this designation: An evangelist is someone who shares the good news of Jesus Christ and His kingdom. In the two passages of Scripture mentioned above, only Philip – one of the deacons in Acts 6:5 – is actually called an evangelist. Philip had grown in grace and was transformed from a deacon to a fully empowered preacher of the good news (Acts 8:5-7). After being called by the Lord to meet the treasurer and subsequently baptize him, he disappeared from the place, found himself in Ashdod, and wandered about (Acts 8:39f.). This description makes it clear that the ministry of the evangelist is not tied to a local church.

My personal experience with evangelists confirms this assumption. Character-wise, they are often quite proactive personalities who are quick to start conversations and make connections. Evangelists have a special love for people who do not believe in Jesus. They are passionate about meeting new people and getting new impressions. Evangelists see the lostness of people and hear the heartbeat of God. They are usually very communicative. They can talk to strangers about Jesus Christ with little effort. They tend to have a positive clarity and are able to explain the gospel in a simple and lively way. Their ministry is validated by visible acts of God (Acts 8:6).

With their passion for people, they have a contagious effect on others in their environment. They are able to constantly remind the congregation of their mission and motivate them to carry it out (Mt. 28:19f.). This ministry is very important because there are always situations in which churches neglect this assignment. When they lack evangelists, they run the risk of focusing on themselves and not on those whom God still wants to reach. Everyone is capable of leading people to Jesus, but that does not automatically mean that God has given us the office of evangelist.

The evangelist, like the apostle and the prophet, must also expect to be criticized for having a certain distance from the people in the congregation. This is due to different circumstances. Firstly, his ministry is not tied to a particular place. In addition, he tries to connect with many people in his environment. Therefore, his time budget for the brothers and sisters in the church can only be tight. Furthermore, it is sometimes said that evangelists have little understanding of the other tasks in the church.

11.5 SHEPERDS

We already read about shepherds in the Old Testament. Princes are also referred to as such (e.g., in Mic. 5:4 and Jer. 3:15). Their task was to take care of the people of God. The good shepherd of the famous Psalm 23 is also worth mentioning, which gives us the image of the caring God. Finally, Jeremiah also promises a special guardian sent by God to His people (Jer. 23:4f.). Jesus calls himself the "good shepherd", and Jeremiah's promise is thus clearly related to Him (Jn. 10:14; 1 Pet. 2:25). Jesus commissioned the apostles to shepherd the people (Jn. 21:15-17), and Paul commissioned the elders of the early churches (Acts 20:28). The shepherding ministry is associated with the ministry of the elders, so we can assume that it is bound to a place for the long term.
Unlike the previous three offices, his sphere of influence is not national. He takes care of the local congregation.
The Bible provides some criteria for the selection of elders, which in turn provides insight into the shepherding ministry (1 Tim. 3:1-11; Tit. 1:6-9). Peter also mentions how they are to carry out their ministry (1 Pet. 5:1-4): They should to be trustworthy and exemplary. Despite these conditions, it remains relatively open how we are to imagine their exact activity or the way in which they carry out their ministry. It can be assumed that shepherds, along with other ministries, are the local leaders and assistants who work for the good of the community and the individual.

A shepherd is caring, according to the example given by Christ Himself as the guardian of His sheep (1 Pet. 5:2). He is not only seen as the person to turn to in case of sickness or need (Jas. 5:14), but he also keeps an eye on the whole flock and bears the responsibility for it (Heb. 13:17). He cares about good fellowship. He reaches out to individuals in the church and listens to them. It is his heart's desire to see that the sheep are well supplied with all that they need. A shepherd is certainly also a good pastor who takes enough time for the brothers and sisters. He gladly accepts hardship for the good of others (Jn. 10:11).

Without the shepherd, the church lacks a leader who is aware of and responsive to the individual. The ministries that go beyond the church cannot do what a shepherd can do with his budget of time and gifts on the spot. Because he cares so much for the people, his ministry is focused on them. As a result, he is in danger of losing sight of everything outside the church: The relationships and peace of the church, for example, can become too distracting to focus on extending the kingdom of God.

11.6 Teacher

The term teacher is a ministry term that is frequently used in the New Testament. It was very common in the religious environment of early Christianity. Among other things, Jesus is very often referred to as a teacher. Many times, he publicly interpreted the Scriptures and also criticized the interpretations of the other scholars (e.g. the Pharisees). Unlike the educated Jewish elite of his day, he taught with the authority of the Holy Spirit (Matt. 7:28f.) and helped the people find a living connection to the ancient Scriptures.

Jesus also transferred the mission of teaching to his disciples (Mt. 28:20; Mk. 6:30). Early on, a special talent for teaching emerged in some of them (Acts 13:1; Acts 18:24). Obviously, their main task was to interpret the Torah and pass on the teachings of Jesus (2 Tim. 1:11). One of these men who was well versed in the Scriptures was Apollos. He is more often referred to as a teacher in literature today, although he is not specifically identified as such in the New Testament testimony. However, the description of his person in Acts 18:24-28 leaves little doubt about his calling: With a letter of recommendation, he traveled from Ephesus to Achaia and later to Corinth, where he had a formative ministry (1 Cor. 1:12; 3:6). It can be assumed that Apollos also had a kind of itinerant ministry because of his office (Tit. 3:13).

A teacher is a minister who is not necessarily tied to one place. Certainly, he has a kind of home church to which he is obliged to belong. But depending on the nature of his ministry, he may also be invited by other churches.

The office of a teacher carries a lot of responsibility (Jas. 3:1), so he should also show a certain maturity, similar to Apollos. Who is described as an eloquent and educated man. A teacher must be familiar with the biblical foundations so that he can lay a solid foundation and give stability to the church. He is fascinated by unraveling the connections and depths of the Word of God. Research gives him joy. The ability to present complicated issues in an understandable way is one of his great strengths. Therefore, a teacher is known for his sharp mind and plausible reasoning.

Without him, a congregation is in danger of believing and following false teachings. This danger will never be eliminated even with all the tools and books that exist today.

A teacher is a person who moves among people and also cultivates a certain closeness to the congregation – after all, he is interested in the development of individual brothers and sisters. A great weakness of teachers, however, is that they tend to become petty, controlling, corrective, and distant from the congregation. Their study of the Scriptures can also become an end in itself if they lose sight of the real task of equipping the church.

1.   God works in the world through people. How do you view leaders in church congregations?

2.   We see that leaders are called to different ministries. Yet many Christians have a desire for a leader to have a lot of skills. Has this chapter changed your view of leaders?

3.   Which of these ministries speak to you personally the most? Perhaps one of the ministries catches your special attention or preference. This could be an indication that the Lord is calling you in a similar way.

12 Outlook

Philip, the evangelist, is a biblical figure who has always impressed me very much: He enters the stage of the New Testament as a deacon (Acts 6:5). His first activity that we learn of is of an organizational nature. For when the apostles discover that they cannot do what they are gifted to do, Philip agrees to wait on tables in their place. Although the apostles insisted that this task be performed by Spirit-filled people, few today would probably think that this could be considered a spiritual ministry. Most believers want to follow a spiritual calling. But as a pastor, I know that it is not always easy to find people for some of the seemingly mundane tasks in the church. Philip, on the other hand, does not think of himself as too important, and he is faithful in carrying out his duties. In this context, he has the perfect opportunity to share the good news (Acts 6:7). Later in Acts 8:6, we meet him as a mature evangelist whose ministry is accompanied by signs and wonders. Philip is a good example of growth in the grace of God. He is willing to do the ministry for which his leaders have chosen him. But he grows in grace and God expands his territory (Acts 8:40).

The New Testament speaks a lot about the growth of believers (e.g., 2 Cor. 9:10; 10:15; 1 Thess. 3:12; 2 Thess. 1:3; Heb. 5:12-14). Peter's final words in 2 Peter 3:18 are especially memorable:

But grow in the grace and knowledge of our Lord and Savior Jesus Christ. To Him be glory now and forevermore! Amen

I am convinced that the grace of God can grow and increase in the lives of believers – like everything else in creation. This is true for all the charisms and gifts that I have covered! And it is my belief that this is entirely in the mind of the Creator. But at this point, man is also challenged to cooperate.

Lack of willingness is certainly not the reason why most of them do not grow in grace. It is more likely due to the fact that we do not know how to encourage this growth. Therefore, at the end of this book, I would like to describe in a few words a possible way to bring grace to its fullest in our lives.

12.1 THREE STEPS

When I look at our potential for growth, I like to talk about the "possibilities of God." At the end of the day, it is a matter of entering into the plan that He has prepared for us and not of achieving what we want in the first place. It may be a surprise to some, but unlike many others, I am not a believer in leaving your comfort zone. Instead, I believe it's about expanding your comfort zone. By learning new things, it becomes the familiar and thus a safe zone in which we can move effortlessly.

What we have is not despicable, so we do not have to leave it behind. Instead, we should reconcile with our past, gratefully accept what we have, and expand our territory. This is the way to a healthy present. If, on the other hand, we try to be someone we are not, it will only lead to further complications. Reconciled with our past, we can offer to God what we already have. In the Chassidic stories, a certain Rabbi Alexander says: "Man does not like to use broken vessels. Not so God, for all His servants are broken vessels, as the Scripture says: "The LORD is near to the brokenhearted, and He helps those who are crushed in spirit." (Ps. 34:19)

Living in this healthy, reconciled present enables us to create a hopeful future that becomes a reality with the Lord.

These steps are certainly not easy, especially when our own past is eating at us. But there are always things to be grateful for. What's done is done, and we must learn to make peace with it. When we experience pain, we should work to receive healing. It does not do any good to recall the pain over and over again and relive it in our minds. In doing so, we only interfere with the healing process. If we give bad experiences the power to disrupt our lives, the past can hold our future hostage. Conversely, it is difficult for the grateful person to be anxious at the same time!

Let us look ahead to the possibilities of God and let us wait for the future full of faith in the action of His grace. A vision is certainly far from the present, and those who wish to realize it do not know exactly if and how it will be realized. But the journey to a distant place begins with a first step. It begins when we walk, not when we talk about it.

12.2 OVERCOMING PAIN

In chapter 5 I used Plato's allegory of the cave to explain that development is always associated with pain. The new and unknown is conquered through a difficult process. Every time I started working in a new area, I had to accept failure. There was much I could not do, and some things were simply unknown to me. Anyone who attends a training session at a soccer club for the first time is likely to be smiled at by the other participants. He will have to hear that the cobbler should stick to his last and much more. But if he has a little talent and motor skills, it will show sooner or later if he continues training. Talent alone is not enough; it must be developed. We need knowledge and experience to perform well.

One mistake I often see people make when entering new areas is to retreat as soon as the first growing pains set in. For some, the process of development is too strenuous. Others shy away from the criticism, rejection, and stares of others, so they retreat into the safe and familiar.

With diligence, effort, and the grace of the Lord, these growing pains can be overcome. However, there is another key that can help us not get stuck at this point: A suitable leader or mentor. People who have walked the path before us can be a tremendous asset in this process. They know the pitfalls and mistakes to avoid, and they can foresee the possibilities of God.

As we have seen, the purpose of the fivefold ministry is to equip the saints. Therefore, it only makes sense to consult with a leader who is willing to do this. Ideally, this would be a companion who has a similar calling. He sees things we have not yet discovered and

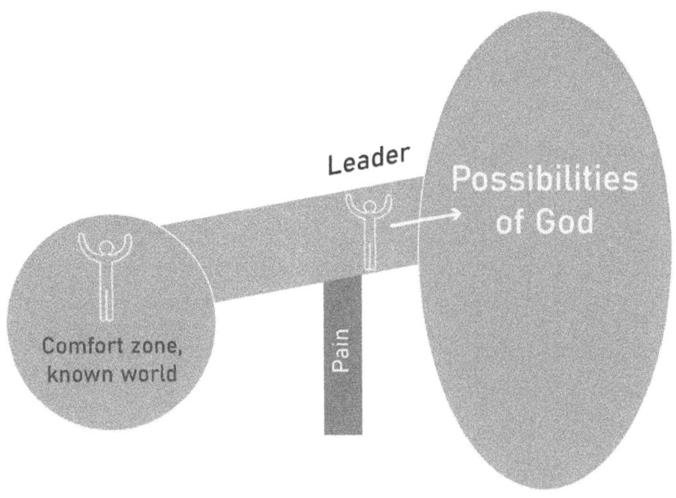

knows how to overcome certain obstacles. In this way, he helps us to overcome the limitations of our thinking, to see God's vision, and to grow toward it. We don't have to have the same leader at every stage of our life, but we should always have someone at our side to walk alongside.

Those who take the risk to expand their familiar waters with an experienced sailor at their side, and who are willing to seek what the Lord has prepared for them, will see how they grow in grace. In this way, God's kingdom will become a little more real with you here on earth.

WE DO NOT BUILD THE KINGDOM OF GOD TO LIVE,

BUT WE LIVE TO BUILD THE KINGDOM OF GOD.

BIBLIOGRAPHY

Achtemeier, P.J.: *1 Peter: a commentary on First Peter*. Minneapolis 1996.

Augustinus, Aurelius: *Des heiligen Kirchenvaters Aurelius Augustinus Vorträge über das Evangelium des hl. Johannes. Vorträge 1–23. Bibliothek der Kirchenväter*. Kempten 1913.

Baumert, Norbert: *Sorgen des Seelsorgers. Übersetzung und Auslegung des ersten Korintherbriefs*. Würzburg 2007.

Bickle, Mike / Sullivant, Michael: *Prophetie oder Profilneurose. Wie die Gabe der Prophetie in unseren Gemeinden reifen kann*. Aßlar 1996.

Brunner, Emil: *Gnade, in: Religion in Geschichte und Gegenwart 3. Band 2*. Tübingen 1957.

Fee, Gordon: *Der Geist Gottes und die Gemeinde. Eine Einladung, Paulus ganz neu zu lesen*. Erzhausen 2005.

Fee, Gordon: *God's empowering presence: the Holy Spirit in the letters of Paul*. Grand Rapids, Michigan 2011.

Greshake, Gisbert: *Gnade – Geschenk der Freiheit*. Kevelaer 2004.

Grudem, Wayne: *Die Gabe der Prophetie*. Nürnberg 1994.

Härle, Wilfried: *Dogmatik*. Berlin 2012.

Hauck, Friedrich / Schwinge Gerhard: *Theologisches Fach- und Fremdwörterbuch*. Göttingen 2005.

Kaldewey, Jens: *Die starke Hand Gottes: Der fünffältige Dienst*. Oberweningen 2001.

Karcher, Günther: *Pneumatologie II*. Erzhausen 2007.

Maxwell, John C.: Charakter und Charisma. *Die 21 wichtigsten Qualitäten erfolgreicher Führungspersönlichkeiten*. Gießen 2005.

Mehrabian, Albert: *Inference of Attitude from Nonverbal Communication in Two Channels. In: The Journal of Counselling Psychology 31.* S. 248–252, 1967.

Moltmann, Jürgen: *Der Geist des Lebens. Eine ganzheitliche Pneumatologie*. Gütersloh 1991.

Roth, Ulli: *Gnadenlehre*. Paderborn 2013.

Rust, Heinrich Christian: *Prophetisch leben – prophetisch dienen. Die Entdeckung einer vergessenen Gabe*. Witten 2014.

Schnackenburg, Rudolf / Schweizer Eduard: *Evangelisch-katholischer Kommentar Zum Neuen Testament. Der Brief an die Epheser / Der Brief an die Kolosser*. Ostfildern 2013.

Schniewind, Julius: *Das biblische Wort von der Bekehrung. Berlin 1971*.

Schrage, Wolfgang: *Evangelisch-katholischer Kommentar Zum Neuen Testament. Der erste Brief an die Korinther*. Ostfildern 2015.

Schulz von Thun, Friedemann: *Miteinander reden 1: Störungen und Klärungen: Allgemeine Psychologie der Kommunikation*. Hamburg 2011.

Steer, Roger: *Georg Müller. Vertraut mit Gott*. Bielefeld 2009.

Turner, Max: *The Holy Spirit and spiritual gifts: in the New Testament church and today*. Peabody, Massachusetts 2009.

Ulonska, Reinhold: *Geistesgaben in Lehre und Praxis. Der Umgang mit den Charismen des Heiligen Geistes*. Erzhausen 2003.

Ulonska, Reinhold: *Gott hat gesetzt... Auftrag und Aufgabe der charismatischen Ämter*. Erzhausen 1995.

Vatter, Stefan: Finden, fördern, freisetzen: Wirksam führen – die Wiederentdeckung des apostolischen Dienstes. Schwarzenfeld 2016.

Westermann, Claus: *A Continental Commentary: Genesis 1–11*. Minneapolis 1994.

Wolff, Hans Walter: Anthropologie des Alten Testaments. Gütersloh 2010.

www.ingramcontent.com/pod-product-compliance
Lightning Source LLC
LaVergne TN
LVHW051053180726
843512LV00019B/1453

Il est huit heures du matin et je suis à la gare routière de Paris, en France.	It's eight in the morning and I'm at the bus station in Paris, in France.
5 Je viens d'arriver après trente heures de bus. Trente heures ! Le bon côté des choses, c'est que maintenant je suis loin de mes parents, qui sont pénibles.	I just got here after thirty hours on the bus. Thirty hours! The good thing is that now I am very far from my parents, who are a real pain.
10 Demain, je vais à Toulouse pour rendre visite à ma meilleure amie qui y vit maintenant, mais aujourd'hui, je 15 vais faire du tourisme à Paris.	Tomorrow, I am going to Toulouse to visit my best friend who lives there now, but today I am going to go sightseeing in Paris.
Paris est la capitale de la France et il y a beaucoup de choses que je veux voir. 20	Paris is the capital of France and there are many things I want to see.
Je dois aller à l'office du tourisme pour demander un plan, mais d'abord je dois aller aux toilettes. 25	I have to go to the tourist office to ask for a map, but first I need to go to the bathroom.
Je vais aux toilettes de l'autre côté de la gare. L'office du tourisme s'y trouve aussi.	I go towards the toilets on the other side of the station. The tourist office is there too.
30 Il y a beaucoup de gens à la gare routière.	There are a lot of people at the station.

Elle est très fréquentée et bruyante. Tous les gens semblent très sérieux et très occupés.

5

Je pense à mes parents : — Je n'ai pas besoin d'eux, ils sont vraiment pénibles. Ce que je veux, c'est être indépendante.

10

Il fait une chaleur d'enfer à Paris. J'ai un peu mal à la tête à cause du bruit et de la chaleur.

15 J'ai également mal à l'estomac car, en vérité, je n'ai pas mangé grand-chose ces trente dernières heures.

20 J'arrive aux toilettes, mais avant d'y entrer, j'ai besoin de boire de l'eau. Je me souviens que j'ai une bouteille d'eau dans mes bagages.

25

Soudain, je suis stupéfiée.

— Mes bagages !

30 Mes bagages sont toujours dans le bus.

It is very busy and there is a lot of noise. All the people seem very serious and very busy.

I think of my parents: *I don't need them; they are really annoying. What I want is to be independent.*

It is deathly hot in Paris. My head hurts a little from the noise and the heat.

My stomach also hurts because, in truth, I haven't eaten much in the last thirty hours.

I get to the toilets, but before entering, I need to drink water. I remember that I have a bottle of water in my luggage.

Suddenly, I freeze like a statue.

My luggage!

My luggage is still on the bus.

J'ai laissé mes bagages dans le bus ! C'est impossible !

I have left my luggage on the bus! It can't be!

Je commence à courir et je ne
5   m'arrête pas avant d'avoir atteint l'arrêt de bus.

I start running and don't stop until I get to the bus stop.

J'ai besoin de mes bagages ; mes vêtements et mon
10   passeport sont dans le sac !

I need my luggage; my clothes and my passport are inside the bag!

Je vois le bus commencer à quitter l'arrêt de bus. J'essaie de courir plus vite.
15

I see how the bus starts to leave the stop. I try to run faster.

Je crie au chauffeur : « S'il vous plaît ! Attendez ! Attendez ! Attendeeeez ! Mes bagages !! »

I shout to the driver: "Please! Wait! Wait! Waiiiiiit! My luggage!!"

20   Mais le chauffeur ne m'entend pas. J'essaie de suivre le bus, mais une voiture me renverse presque.

But the driver doesn't hear me. I try to follow the bus, but a car almost runs me over.

25   Effrayée, je m'arrête dans la rue ; j'ai le souffle court, je n'arrive pas à respirer.

Scared, I stop in the street; I'm short of breath, I can't breathe.

Je n'arrive pas à le croire !
30

I cannot believe it!

J'ai laissé mes bagages dans le bus.

I have left my luggage on the bus.

Maintenant je n'ai pas de
passeport, pas de vêtements,
rien.

5 Quelle idiote ! Je suis à cinq
minutes de mes parents et je
perds mes bagages.

— Attention, mademoiselle !
10 crie un homme âgé depuis le
trottoir.

J'entends quelque chose.
Je me retourne et je vois un
15 autre bus.

Je me déplace rapidement et
grimpe sur le trottoir, où le vieil
homme me regarde.
20
— Tu n'es pas d'ici, n'est-ce
pas, ma fille ? me demande
l'homme.

25 Il est plus petit que moi et tient
un magnifique chat dans ses
bras.

Je pense que c'est un chat
30 persan, comme celui de ma
mère.

Now I have no passport, no
clothes, nothing.

*I am so dumb! Five minutes
away from my parents and I
lose my luggage.*

"Careful, miss!" Shouts an
older man from the sidewalk.

I hear something.
I turn and see another bus.

I move quickly and climb onto
the pavement, where the older
man looks at me.

"You're not from here, are you,
my dear?" The man asks me.

He is shorter than me and has a
beautiful cat in his arms.

I think it is a Persian cat, like
my mother's.

Je lui dis que je ne viens pas de Paris, que je suis allemande et que je vis à la campagne, près de Berlin.

5

— Eh bien, puisque tu es à Paris, tu devrais essayer les pains au chocolat, dit l'homme avec un sourire.

10

Il porte un costume chic, mais il est usé, et le chat porte un bandana autour du cou.

15

C'est une vision plutôt étrange.

— Les pains au chocolat sont une spécialité française, me dit-il. Je m'appelle Michel, au fait.

20

— Merci beaucoup, Michel, je lui dis, — et quel curieux chat tu as...

25

Michel rit.

— Haha... elle est très curieuse, oui... Son nom est Madame de Pompadour.

30

I tell him that I am not from Paris, that I am German and that I live in the countryside near Berlin.

"Well, since you're in Paris, you should try the *pains au chocolat*", says the man with a smile.

He's wearing a fancy suit, but it's worn out, and the cat is wearing a bandana around its neck.

It's a pretty strange sight.

"*Pains au chocolat* are a French specialty," he tells me. "By the way, I'm Michel."

"Thank you very much, Michel," I tell him, "and what an interesting cat you have ..."

Michel laughs.

"Haha ... she's very interesting, yes ... Her name is Madame de Pompadour."

— Ah, excuse-moi, je ne savais pas que c'était une dame ! Je suis Joanna, au fait. Enchantée de te rencontrer.

5

Michel me fait ses adieux et en les regardant marcher dans la rue.

10 Je pense à sa recommandation des pains au chocolat.

Je vois un café juste à côté de 15 l'office du tourisme.

J'arrive au café et je m'assois à une table. J'ai très faim et très soif.
20
J'ai besoin de boire et de quelque chose à manger. Je regarde le menu.

25 Il y a beaucoup de plats délicieux et beaucoup de boissons aussi.

Il y a des croque-monsieurs, 30 des quiches, des pizzas, des sandwichs, des hamburgers et des frites.

"Oh, excuse me, I didn't know it was a lady! By the way, I'm Joanna. Nice to meet you."

Michel says goodbye to me and as I watch them go down the street.

I think about his recommendation of *pains au chocolat.*

I see a cafe right next to the tourist office.

I get to the cafe and sit at a table. I am very hungry and very thirsty.

I need to drink and to eat something. I look at the menu.

There are many delicious dishes and many drinks too.

There are croque-monsieurs, quiches, pizzas, sandwiches, hamburgers and chips.

Pour boire, je peux choisir entre un chocolat chaud ou un jus d'orange ou un jus de citron ou un jus de pastèque ou un jus d'abricot.	To drink, I can choose between hot chocolate or orange juice or lemon or watermelon or apricot juice.
Je n'ai jamais vu autant de variétés de jus dans ma vie !	I have never seen so many varieties of juice in my life!
Je décide de prendre un pain au chocolat – la recommandation de Michel - et un jus d'orange. Je cherche mon portefeuille dans la poche de ma veste.	I decide to have a *pain au chocolat* - Michel's recommendation - and an orange juice. I search for the wallet in my jacket pocket.
Où est-il ? Il n'est pas là. Je le cherche comme une folle dans les poches de mon pantalon. Rien. J'ai mon téléphone, mais mon portefeuille a disparu.	*Where is it?* It's not there. I look for it like crazy in the pockets of my trousers. Nothing. I have my phone, but my wallet has gone.
Soudain, j'ai le vertige. Je me sens mal. J'ai mal à la tête et je ne me sens pas bien.	Suddenly I feel dizzy. I feel awful. My head hurts and I don't feel well.
Je ne trouve pas mon portefeuille parce qu'il est dans mon bagage. Et mes bagages sont dans le bus.	*I cannot find my wallet because it is in my luggage. And my luggage is on the bus.*
Je suis si bête !	*I'm so dumb!*

The line numbers printed in the left margin are: 5, 10, 15, 20, 25, 30.

Maintenant, je n'ai pas de vêtements, pas de passeport et pas d'argent. Je n'ai pas non plus ma carte de crédit.

5

Je veux manger un pain au chocolat et boire un jus d'orange, mais je ne peux pas parce que je n'ai pas d'argent.

10

Que vais-je faire ?

Il est huit heures et demie du matin et je suis dans une grande ville que je ne connais pas, sans argent et sans logement.

15

Je sors mon téléphone portable. Je ne veux pas appeler mes parents, mais peut-être que mon amie à Toulouse peut m'aider.

20

Je tape son numéro de téléphone et je l'appelle. Oui, je suis sûr que ma meilleure amie va m'aider et que tout ira bien.

25

Je n'ai pas besoin de ma famille. J'attends cinq secondes ... dix secondes ... et finalement l'appel se connecte.

30

Now I have no clothes, no passport and no money. I don't have my credit card either.

I want to eat a *pain au chocoat* and drink an orange juice, but I can't because I don't have money.

What am I going to do?

It is eight thirty in the morning and I am in a big city, which I do not know, without money and without accommodation.

I take out my mobile phone. I don't want to call my parents, but maybe my friend in Toulouse can help me.

I type in her phone number and call her. Yes, surely my best friend is going to help me and everything will be fine.

I don't need my family.
I wait five seconds ... ten seconds ... and finally the call connects.

À l'autre bout de la ligne, une voix électronique dit :
— Bienvenue chez Orange. Votre téléphone n'a pas de crédit. Pour ajouter du crédit, appuyez sur la touche un…

Je crois que je vais vomir. J'ai laissé mes bagages dans le bus.

Je n'ai pas mon passeport, je n'ai pas d'argent et mon téléphone n'a pas de crédit.

Que vais-je faire ?

On the other end of the line, an electronic voice says:
— Welcome to Orange. Your phone has no credit. To add credit press one…

I think I am going to vomit. I have left my luggage on the bus.

I don't have my passport, I don't have money and my phone has no credit.

What am I going to do?

CHAPTER 2

Joanna va à la Place de la Concorde.

Je vais au bureau des objets trouvés. L'homme dit qu'il va envoyer un message au chauffeur de bus.

5

Je lui donne mon numéro de téléphone et l'homme me donne un plan de la ville.

10 Je quitte la station. Il fait super chaud dehors. J'ai besoin de boire de l'eau. Il y a une fontaine en face de la station. Je bois beaucoup d'eau. C'est très
15 rafraîchissant.

Je décide de me promener dans Paris et de retourner au bureau des objets trouvés dans l'après-
20 midi.

Je ne sais pas ce que je vais manger, mais au moins il y a des fontaines où je peux boire.
25 Je ne mourrai pas de soif.

Devant la gare, il y a un énorme rond-point et la circulation est très dense. Il est
30 neuf heures du matin et les rues sont animées.

I go to the lost and found office. The man says that he is going to send a message to the bus driver.

I give him my phone number and the man gives me a map of the city.

I leave the station. It is super hot outside. I need to drink water. There is a fountain opposite the station. I drink a lot of water. It is very refreshing.

I decide to take a walk around Paris and return to the lost and found office in the afternoon.

I don't know what I'm going to eat, but at least there are fountains where I can drink. I won't die of thirst.

In front of the station, there is a huge roundabout and the traffic is very heavy. It's nine in the morning and the streets are busy.

Il y a des voitures, des motos et des bus partout.

There are cars, motorcycles and buses everywhere.

Entre la rue et le trottoir, il y a
5 une voie verte réservée seulement aux vélos. Il y a aussi des gens qui marchent dans toutes les directions.

Between the street and the pavement, there is a green lane that is for bicycles only. There are also people walking in all directions.

10 Je traverse le rond-point et je vois que je suis dans la rue La Fayette. La gare s'appelle Gare du Nord, je décide donc de suivre cette rue pour ne pas me
15 perdre.

I cross the roundabout and see that I am on a street called *La Fayette.* The station is called *Gare du Nord,* so I decide to follow this street so as not to get lost.

Paris est une ville magnifique. Il y a de nombreux bâtiments historiques et des arbres
20 partout.

Paris is a beautiful city. There are many historical buildings and trees everywhere.

— Quelle ville verte !

What a green city!

Je descends la rue La Fayette et
25 après environ trente minutes, j'arrive sur une très grande place.

I go down *La Fayette* street and after about thirty minutes I come to a very large square.

C'est spectaculaire. Elle est
30 vraiment spacieuse et d'une élégance magique.

It is spectacular. It is truly spacious and magically elegant.

Il y a des touristes qui prennent des photos des bâtiments et des enfants qui jouent joyeusement sous les monuments.

There are tourists taking photos of the buildings and children playing happily under the monuments.

5

Je regarde mon plan. Je suis à Place de la Concorde.

I look at my map. I am in the *Place de la Concorde.*

L'arôme délicieux de la

10 nourriture remplit la place. Je regarde autour de moi et vois les nombreux cafés et restaurants qui bordent la place.

The delicious aroma of food fills the square. I look around and see the large number of cafes and restaurants that can be found on the square.

15 Les gens mangent et discutent avec enthousiasme autour des tables.

There are people eating and chatting enthusiastically at the tables.

Je ne me sens pas bien parce

20 que je suis affamée et que je ne sais pas quand je vais manger.

I don't feel very well because I'm starving and I don't know when I'm going to eat.

Si seulement j'avais de l'argent pour profiter de cet endroit.

25 J'aimerais goûter aux plats typiques : le jambon de Paris, les baguettes, les croque-monsieur, la soupe à l'oignon et plus encore.

I wish I had the money to enjoy this place. I would love to try typical dishes: *Paris* ham, baguettes, croque-monsieurs, onion soup and more.

30

J'aimerais aussi goûter les glaces vendues sur la place, mais je ne peux pas.

I would also like to try the ice creams that are on sale in the square, but I can't.

Je n'ai rien, j'ai juste faim et
soif.

Je m'assois à l'une des tables de
5 la place. Je vais peut-être faire
de la peine au serveur ?

Si seulement ! Mais quand le
serveur arrive et que j'explique
10 que je n'ai pas d'argent, il ne
manifeste aucune pitié.

— Tu ne peux pas t'asseoir ici
si tu ne vas rien acheter, me dit
15 le serveur.

— Très bien, monsieur.
Pardon. Je dis et je me lève.

20 Je vais à la fontaine pour boire
plus d'eau. Que puis-je faire
d'autre ? Je suis assise sur la
place et un touriste me voit.

25 Il est américain, mais il
ressemble beaucoup à mon
père. Il dit à sa femme en
anglais :
— So sad to see so many young
30 people on the streets, isn't it
honey?

I have nothing, just my hunger
and thirst.

I sit at one of the tables in the
square. Maybe the waiter will
feel sorry for me?

I wish! But when the waiter
comes and I explain that I have
no money, he does not feel
sorry at all.

"You can't sit here if you're not
going to buy anything," the
waiter tells me.

"Okay, sir. Sorry," I say and
get up.

I go to the fountain to drink
more water. What else can I
do? I sit in the square and a
tourist sees me.

He is American, but he looks a
lot like my father. He says to
his wife in English:

—*So sad to see so many young
people on the streets, isn't it
honey?*

L'Américain me donne
cinquante centimes. J'ai
tellement honte, mais je ne
peux pas refuser. C'est le seul
5   argent que j'ai.

The American gives me fifty
cents. I am so ashamed, but I
cannot refuse them. It is the
only money I have.

Je fixe la pièce, soupire et me
dirige avec avidité vers le
kiosque.
10

I stare at the coin, sigh and
walk hungrily to the kiosk.

Avec cinquante centimes, je ne
peux acheter qu'une sucette
Pierrot Gourmand.

With fifty cents the only thing I
can buy is a *Pierrot Gourmand*
lollipop.

15   — Je n'ai pas un sou !

I'm absolutely penniless!

Je passe une heure ou plus sur
la place à observer les touristes
qui savourent leurs repas.
20

I spend an hour or more in the
square watching the tourists
enjoying their meals.

Finalement, je décide de
retourner au bureau des objets
perdus. L'homme dans le
bureau dit que mes bagages ont
25   disparu.

In the end I decide to go back
to the lost property office. The
man in the office says my
luggage is missing.

Il dit qu'il m'appellera
immédiatement si mes bagages
sont retrouvés.

He says that he will call me
immediately if my luggage
shows up.

Soudain, je me mets à pleurer. Je n'en peux plus. J'ai chaud, j'ai faim et je ne me sens pas bien.	Suddenly, I start crying. I can't bear it anymore. I'm hot, I'm hungry, and I'm not feeling well.
Je veux retourner chez moi en Allemagne.	I want to go back to my hometown in Germany.
Je ne m'entends pas avec mes parents, mais vivre avec eux est mieux que de vivre seule dans la rue.	I don't get along with my parents, but living with them is better than living alone on the streets.
L'homme du bureau des objets trouvés est surpris : — Vous allez bien, mademoiselle ?	The man from the lost property office is shocked. "Are you okay, miss?"
J'explique que je ne vais pas bien et que j'ai peur d'être seule dans une grande ville que je ne connais pas.	I explain that I am not OK and that I am afraid of being alone in a big city that I do not know.
L'homme dans le bureau a un regard inquiet. Je me demande s'il a des enfants.	The man in the office looks worried. I wonder if he himself has children.
Je pense à mon père : — Que fait-il maintenant ? J'ai quitté la maison sans rien dire. Mon père doit être très inquiet, ma mère aussi.	I think of my father. *What is he doing now?* I left home without saying anything. My father must be very worried; my mother too.

L'homme du bureau me tend
une brique de jus de fruits.
C'est délicieux.
— Écoute, petite, dit l'homme
5 du bureau, il y a un endroit près
de la Rue de Rivoli.

L'homme du bureau prend mon
plan et met un « X » sur Le
10 Jardin des Tuileries.
— Ce n'est pas loin d'ici et tu
peux y dormir. Ce n'est pas le
Ritz, mais c'est un endroit sûr.

The man in the office gives me
a carton of juice.
It is delicious.
"Listen, child," says the man in
the office, "there's a place next
to *Rue de Rivoli.*"

The man in the office takes my
map and puts an "X" on the
Jardin des Tuileries.
"It's not far from here and you
can sleep there. It is not the
Ritz, but it is a safe place."

CHAPTER 3

Joanna rencontre Michel.

La Rue de Rivoli est une rue grandiose, large et élégante.	The *Rue de Rivoli* is a grandiose, wide and elegant street.
5 D'un côté de la rue se trouve le Jardin des Tuileries et de l'autre côté, des rangées de bâtiments historiques.	On one side of the street is the *Jardin des Tuileries* and on the other side are rows of historic buildings.
10 Il est déjà huit heures du soir. Mes douze premières heures à Paris ont été problématiques...	It's already eight in the evening. My first twelve hours in Paris have been problematic...
Je me trouve maintenant devant 15 un magnifique bâtiment qui semble très important. Le panneau dit : Musée du Louvre.	Now I am in front of a magnificent building that seems very important. The sign says: *Musée du Louvre.*
20 Je reconnais le nom. Il s'agit de l'un des musées d'art les plus célèbres et les plus prestigieux du monde.	I recognise the name. It is one of the most famous and prestigious art museums in the world.
25 J'aimerais beaucoup visiter le musée et profiter des œuvres d'art, mais sans argent, je ne peux pas.	I would very much like to visit the museum and enjoy the works of art, but without money, I can't.
30 De l'autre côté du Musée du Louvre se trouve une arche magnifique.	On the other side of the *Musée du Louvre* there is a magnificent arch.

Je vois qu'elle s'appelle l'Arc
de Triomphe du Carroussel.

Je regarde le plan que l'homme
5 du bureau des objets perdus m'a
donné. Le « X » est proche de
l'arche.

Je vois un groupe de tentes sur
10 le trottoir. Est-ce un camp au
milieu de la ville ?

Il y a des gens qui discutent,
assis par terre ou sur de vieilles
15 chaises. Ces gens ont l'air sales,
sauvages et intimidants.
— J'ai peur.

Il me semble que c'est l'endroit
20 que l'homme du bureau des
objets perdus a mentionné.

Mais ce n'est pas possible. Je ne
peux pas camper avec des
25 étrangers au milieu de la ville !

Je regarde de nouveau vers le
Musée du Louvre.

I see that it's called *Arc de
Triomphe du Carroussel.*

I look at the map the man in the
lost property office gave me.
The "X" is close to the arch.

I see a group of tents on the
pavement. *Is it a camp in the
middle of the city?*

There are people chatting,
sitting on the floor or in old
chairs. Those people seem
dirty, wild and intimidating.
I'm afraid.

It looks like this is the site the
man from the lost and found
office mentioned.

But it can't be. *I can't camp
with strangers in the middle of
the city!*

I look at the *Musée du Louvre*
again.

Il y a des gens élégants qui
sortent d'une exposition d'art.

Je pense que je veux être avec
5   eux, je veux dîner avec eux, je
veux rester avec eux.

— Mais que puis-je faire ?

10 Je me demande si je peux les
approcher et demander une
chambre avec petit-déjeuner
inclus. Mais je ne peux pas.

15 Je me sens complètement seule
et perdue.

Je ne suis pas une mendiante !

20 Je prends une grande
inspiration pour ne pas pleurer.
Soudain, j'entends une voix :
— Mademoiselle !
Mademoiselle ! Mademoiselle !
25 Joanna !

Je tourne la tête et je vois un
homme âgé qui traverse la rue.

30 Il marche en boitant et tient son
chat dans ses bras.

There are some elegant people
coming out of an art exhibition.

I think about how I want to be
with them, I want to dine with
them, I want to stay with them.

But what can I do?

I wonder if I could approach
them and ask for a room with
breakfast included.
But I can't.

I feel completely alone and
lost.

I'm not a beggar!

I take a deep breath to keep me
from crying.
Suddenly, I hear a voice:
"Miss! Miss!
Miss! Joanna!"

I turn my head and see an older
man crossing the street.

He walks whilst limping and
holds his cat in his arms.

C'est l'homme que j'ai rencontré
à la gare !

Il me salue avec un grand
sourire, mais le chat ne semble
pas très heureux de me voir...

— Comment vas-tu, Joanna ?
dit-il. Comment trouves-tu les
pains au chocolat ? Délicieux,
n'est-ce pas ?

Je ne sais pas quoi dire. Je n'ai
pas mangé de pains au
chocolat. En fait, la seule chose
que j'ai mangée de toute la
journée est une sucette.

J'ai faim, j'ai soif, j'ai mal à la
tête, j'ai mal aux jambes et j'ai
envie de pleurer.

L'homme, Michel, me regarde
avec un visage aimable.

Il ressemble à un grand-père
bienveillant, mais il a aussi l'air
fatigué et fragile, et le costume
élégant qu'il porte est vieux et
sale.

— Tu vas bien, ma fille ? dit-il.

It's the man I met at the station!

He greets me with a wide
smile, but the cat doesn't seem
very happy to see me...

"How are you, Joanna?" He
says. "How about the *pains au
chocolat*? Delicious, right?"

I do not know what to say. I
have not eaten *pains au
chocolat*. In fact, the only thing
I've eaten all day is a lollipop.

I'm hungry, I'm thirsty, my
head hurts, my legs hurt, and I
want to cry.

The man, Michel, looks at me
with a kind face.

He is like a good-natured
grandfather, but he also seems
tired and frail, and the elegant
suit he wears is old and dirty.

"Are you okay, child?" he says.

— Écoute, on t'emmène à ton hôtel, Madame de Pompadour et moi ? Tu dois bien dormir et demain tout ira mieux.

"Listen, can we take you to your hotel, Madame de Pompadour and I? You have to sleep well and tomorrow everything will be better."

Je le regarde et je secoue la tête.

I look at him and shake my head.

Je lui dis que je n'ai nulle part où dormir et aussi pas d'argent pour manger.

I tell him that I have nowhere to sleep and that I also have no money to eat.

Je lui dis que je suis seule dans la ville et que je ne sais pas quoi faire.

I tell him that I am alone in the city and that I do not know what to do.

— Ce n'est pas possible, répond Michel. Une fille seule dans la ville... C'est terrible !

"It can't be," Michel replies. "A girl alone in the city... How awful!"

Puis il se tourne vers son chat et lui dit :
— Hé, Madame de Pompadour, que dirais-tu d'inviter Joanna chez nous pour un dîner spécial ?

Then he turns to his cat and says:
"Hey, Madame de Pompadour, what if we invite Joanna to our house for a special dinner?"

— Qu'en penses-tu Joanna ?

"What do you think Joanna?"

Je ne sais pas quoi dire. Je ne pense pas que ce soit une bonne idée d'aller chez un inconnu, mais Michel est très gentil et je n'ai pas d'autre choix.

I do not know what to say. I don't think that it is a good idea to go to the house of an unknown man, but Michel is very kind and I have no other option.

Sentant mon hésitation, Michel indique le camp. — C'est là, ma maison. Mes amis sont là aussi. Viens, je vais te préparer un dîner spécial.

Sensing my doubts, Michel points to the camp. "It's there, my home. My friends are there too. Come, I'm going to cook you a special dinner."

— D'accord ?

"OK?"

— Un dîner spécial ? J'ai tellement faim qu'un morceau de pain rassis serait « spécial » pour moi.

A special dinner? I'm so hungry that a piece of stale bread would be 'special' to me.

— Merci Michel. Tu es très gentil.

"Thank you Michel. You are very kind."

Nous arrivons au camp. Il y a environ une douzaine de tentes et au centre, je vois un groupe de personnes qui discutent et jouent aux cartes.

We arrive at the camp. There are a dozen tents and in the centre, I see a group of people chatting and playing cards.

Ils me regardent avec curiosité.

They look at me with curiosity.

J'ai l'impression que peu de
grandes blondes allemandes
viennent au camp.

— C'est ma nouvelle amie,
Joanna. Elle est allemande, elle
vient d'arriver à Paris et n'a pas
d'argent. Elle va dormir ici ce
soir.

Je me présente aux personnes
du camp. Ils me sourient tous.
Quelqu'un me tend une tasse de
thé. Il est sucré et très
savoureux.

Ces gens ne sont pas des
sauvages, mais ils vivent dans
des conditions quelque peu
insalubres.

L'un des voisins du camp dit
joyeusement :

— Hé, Michel écoute, cette fille
parle très bien français !
Quel bonheur ! Énorme !

— Eh bien, es-tu prête Joanna ?

— Prête ? je répète. Prête pour
quoi ?

I have the impression that not
many tall, blonde German girls
come to camp.

"She's my new friend, Joanna.
She is German, she has just
arrived in Paris and has no
money. She is going to sleep
here tonight."

I introduce myself to the people
from the camp. They all smile
at me. Someone gives me a cup
of tea. It is sweet and very
tasty.

These people are not savages,
but they do live in somewhat
dirty conditions.

One of the camp's neighbours
happily says:

"Hey, listen Michel, this girl
speaks French really well!
What a treat! What a legend!"

"Well, are you ready Joanna?"

Ready? I repeat, "Ready for
what?"

— Pour aller faire les courses, dit Michel en riant.

5 Nous devons trouver les ingrédients pour notre dîner spécial.

"To go shopping," Michel says, laughing.

"We have to look for the ingredients for our special dinner."

CHAPTER 4

Un dîner special.

Il est neuf heures du soir et je
suis dans le centre de Paris
avec Michel et son chat,
Madame de Pompadour.

5

Michel dit qu'il va préparer un
dîner spécial, mais nous avons
besoin d'ingrédients.

10 — Michel, dis-je avec
inquiétude, tu sais que je n'ai
pas d'argent. Je ne peux pas
faire de courses sans argent.

15 Michel sourit et me fait un clin
d'œil.
— Ne t'inquiète pas, ma fille.
J'ai un système.

20 — Un système ? je répète,
encore plus inquiète.

J'espère qu'il ne va pas *voler* les
ingrédients...
25

Nous traversons la rue en
direction de l'Arc de Triomphe
du Carroussel. Puis nous
continuons le long de la Rue de
30 Richelieu.

— Où allons-nous ?

It's nine at night and I'm in the
centre of Paris with Michel and
his cat, Madame de
Pompadour.

Michel says that he is going to
prepare a special dinner, but we
need ingredients.

"Michel," I say worried, "you
know I don't have any money. I
can't go shopping without
money."

Michel smiles and winks at me.

"Don't worry, child. I have a
system."

"A system?" I repeat even more
concerned.

I hope he is not going to *steal*
the ingredients...

We cross the street to *l'Arc de
Triomphe du Carroussel*. Then
we continue along *Rue de
Richelieu*.

Where are we going?

La Rue de Richelieu est très jolie.	*Rue de Richelieu* is very pretty.

La Rue de Richelieu est très
jolie.

Il n'y a pas beaucoup de
5 voitures, mais il y a beaucoup
d'arbres.

C'est très vert et très calme. Des
deux côtés de la rue, on trouve
10 des cafés, des restaurants et des
boutiques. Mon estomac
gargouille.

Nous arrivons à un croisement
15 et l'odeur du pain est tentante.

— Attends ici, Joanna.
Michel me donne le chat, qui
me regarde d'un air méfiant.
20

— Je reviens dans une minute.

Il entre dans un magasin
pendant que Madame de
25 Pompadour et moi regardons la
vitrine.

À l'intérieur, il y a du pain de
toutes les formes : rond, long,
30 grand, petit et moyen. Il y a
aussi des macarons, des
sandwichs et des gâteaux.

Rue de Richelieu is very pretty.

There aren't many cars, but
there are lots of trees.

It is very green and very quiet.
On both sides of the street,
there are cafes, restaurants and
shops. My stomach rumbles.

We come to a junction and the
smell of bread is enticing.

"Wait here, Joanna."
Michel gives me the cat, who
looks at me untrustingly.

"I'll be back in a minute."

He walks into a shop while
Madame de Pompadour and I
look at the shop window.

Inside, there is bread of all
shapes: round, long, large,
small and medium. There are
also macaroons, sandwiches
and cakes.

J'en ai l'eau à la bouche. Je
veux entrer et manger quelque
chose - n'importe quoi, même si
ce ne sont que des miettes -
5 mais je ne peux pas parce que
je n'ai pas d'argent.

Après un moment, Michel sort
du magasin. Il a quelque chose
10 dans ses mains.

Il me regarde et me dit :
— Le pain a l'air bon, n'est-ce
pas ? Tiens, prends ça. Il me
15 tend le sac. Nous devons aller
au prochain endroit.

— Mais... Dis-je confuse.
Qu'est-ce que c'est ?
20

— Qu'est-ce que c'est ?
Michel répète, en prenant le
chat. C'est du pain, bien sûr !

25 — Mais tu n'as pas d'argent non
plus !

Il sourit.
— Tu n'as pas besoin d'argent si
30 tu es intelligent... Il sort une
miche de pain. L'odeur du pain
est trop bonne.

It is making my mouth water. I
want to go in and eat something
- anything, even if it's just
crumbs - but I can't because I
don't have any money.

After a while, Michel leaves
the shop. He has something in
his hands.

He looks at me and says, "The
bread looks good, doesn't it?
Here, take this." He hands me
the bag. "We have to go to the
next place."

"But..." I say confused. "What
is it?"

"What is it?" Michel repeats,
taking the cat. "It's bread, of
course!"

"But you don't have any money
either!"

He smiles.
"You don't need money if
you're smart..." He takes out a
loaf of bread. The smell of the
bread is too good.

— Les gens n'aiment pas le pain moche, ce qui est une bonne chose pour nous. Le boulanger garde le pain moche
5 qu'il ne peut pas vendre et me le donne.
Tu vois qu'il est déformé ?
Je dis oui.

10 Il me donne un morceau de pain et je pense que c'est la chose la plus délicieuse que j'aie jamais mangée de ma vie.

15 — Allons-y, dit Michel.
— Nous avons besoin de plus d'ingrédients.

Ensuite, nous allons dans une
20 charcuterie. Michel entre dans le magasin et Madame de Pompadour et moi regardons dans la vitrine.

25 Il y a des cuisses de jambon partout. Il y a aussi des fromages, des bouteilles d'huile d'olive, des pâtes, des œufs et des saucisses.
30
Une minute plus tard, Michel sort avec un sac rempli de nourriture.

"People don't like *ugly* bread, which is a good thing for us. The baker keeps the *ugly* bread that he cannot sell and gives it to me."

"Do you see it is misshapen?"
I say yes.

He gives me a piece of bread and it seems like the most delicious thing I have ever eaten in my life.

"Come on," Michel says.
"We need more ingredients."

Then we go to a deli. Michel walks into the store and Madame de Pompadour and I look in the shop window.

There are ham legs everywhere. There are also cheeses, bottles of olive oil, pasta, eggs and sausages.

A minute later, Michel comes out with a bag full of food.

Je regarde Michel et il sourit.
— Ce sont les restes qui ne
peuvent pas être vendus. Les
morceaux de jambon et de
5   fromage que personne ne veut
acheter.

— Je n'arrive pas à croire qu'il
y ait autant de nourriture
10   gratuite à Paris !

Je pensais qu'il me faudrait
beaucoup d'argent pour manger
dans cette ville, mais ce n'est
15   pas le cas.

Puis nous allons chez un
marchand de légumes où ils
nous donnent les légumes les
20   plus moches : carottes
déformées, laitue déchirée,
concombres tordus, tomates
meurtries... Toutes les choses
que personne ne veut acheter.
25

Puis nous allons chez le
marchand de fruits et Michel en
ressort avec un sac de bananes,
de pommes, de cerises et de
30   fraises. Il a aussi des abricots et
des oranges.

I look at Michel and he smiles.
"These are the leftovers that
cannot be sold. The pieces of
ham and cheese that nobody
wants to buy."

*It seems incredible to me that
there is so much free food in
Paris!*

I thought that I would need a
lot of money to eat in this city,
but that's not the case.

Then we go to a greengrocer
where they give us the *ugly*
vegetables: deformed carrots,
torn lettuce, bent cucumbers,
bruised tomatoes...
All the things that nobody
wants to buy.

Then we go to the fruit shop
and Michel comes out with a
bag of bananas, apples, cherries
and strawberries. He also has
apricots and oranges.

— Je n'en crois pas mes yeux !	*I can't believe my eyes!*
Finalement, nous allons dans un magasin de vin - et ils nous donnent deux bouteilles de vin ouvertes.	Finally, we go to a wine cellar -a wine shop- and they give us two open bottles of wine.
— Ce sont les bouteilles de dégustation, dit Michel.	"They are the tasting samples" says Michel.
Le chat est assis confortablement sur ses épaules maintenant. A côté du marchand de vin se trouve une poissonnerie.	The cat is sitting comfortably on his shoulders now. Next to the wine cellar there is a fishmonger.
Le propriétaire sort et donne un morceau de poisson à Michel, qui le donne ensuite à Madame de Pompadour.	The owner goes out and gives a piece of fish to Michel, who then gives it to Madame de Pompadour.
Quand le chat a fini son repas, Michel me dit :	When the cat finishes her dinner, Michel says to me:
— On rentre à la maison ?	"Shall we go home?"
Nous avons tellement de sacs que j'ai mal aux doigts à force de les porter, et j'ai mal aux pieds à force d'avoir marché toute la journée.	We have so many bags that my fingers hurt from carrying them, and my feet hurt from walking all day.
Le boitillement de Michel semble pire maintenant aussi.	Michel's limp also looks worse now.

Je me demande :
— Que lui est-il arrivé ? Quelle est son histoire ?

5 Quand nous rentrons au camp, Michel appelle ses amis. Ils se rassemblent tous au centre du camp et allument des bougies.

10 Pour le dîner, nous prenons du pain avec du pâté, de la salade, du jambon, du fromage et du saucisson.

15 Puis, pour le dessert, nous avons toutes sortes de fruits. Je bois de l'eau et Michel boit un verre de vin.

20 Je regarde les visages heureux autour de moi. C'est un dîner spécial. Le dîner le plus délicieux de ma vie. Mais il manque quelque chose...

I wonder: *what could have happened to him?*
What is his story?

When we return to the camp, Michel calls his friends. They all gather in the centre of the camp and light some candles.

For dinner, we have bread with pâté, salad, ham, cheese and *saucisson.*

Then, for dessert, we have all kinds of fruit. I drink water and Michel drinks a glass of wine.

I look at the happy faces around me. It is a special dinner. The most delicious dinner of my life. But something is missing...

CHAPTER 5

Paris gratuit. Le laid est beau.

Je dors dans une tente qui est
libre. Elle a un matelas qui est
un peu petit pour moi, mais au
moins le drap est propre.

5

À ma grande surprise, c'est très
confortable. Je me sens
confortée, presque heureuse.

10 Je suis avec un groupe de
personnes qui s'occupe de moi
et bientôt j'aurai mes bagages.

Je me réveille à huit heures. Il
15 fait chaud dans la tente et
j'entends le bruit de la
circulation.

Il me faut une minute pour
20 réaliser où je suis. Je soupire.
Je suis à Paris, sans argent et je
n'ai toujours pas récupéré mes
bagages.

25 Je m'étire, je me lève et je
quitte la tente. Michel est assis
au centre du camp avec
Madame de Pompadour.

30 — Tu veux un café ? me
demande-t-il.

I sleep in a tent that is free. It
has a thin mattress that is a bit
small for me, but at least the
sheet is clean.

To my surprise it is very
comfortable. I feel upbeat,
almost happy.

I am with a group of people
who are looking after me and
soon I will have my luggage.

I wake up at eight. It is hot in
the tent and I can hear the noise
of the traffic.

It takes me a minute to realise
where I am. I sigh. I am in
Paris, without money and I still
haven't got back my luggage.

I stretch, get up, and leave the
tent. Michel is sitting in the
centre of the camp with
Madame de Pompadour.

"Do you want a coffee?" He
asks me.

— Du café moche ? je réponds
en souriant.

— Les meilleures choses de la
5   vie sont gratuites, dit-il en me
passant une tasse de café.

— Que veux-tu faire
aujourd'hui, Joanna ? As-tu le
10   temps de faire un peu de
tourisme ?

Je hausse les épaules.

15   — Les objets trouvés ne m'ont
pas appelée encore, mais je
veux aller à la gare pour
chercher mes bagages...

20   — Très bien. Madame de
Pompadour et moi venons avec
toi. Si les bagages ne sont pas
là, nous te ferons une visite
guidée de Paris.
25

Savoir que Michel
m'accompagne me permet
d'avoir l'esprit tranquille. Je
trouve même que Madame de
30   Pompadour est plus
sympathique maintenant.

"Ugly coffee?" I answer with a
smile.

"The best things in life are
free," he says, passing me a cup
of coffee.

"What do you want to do today,
Joanna?" Do you have time to
do a little sightseeing?"

I shrug my shoulders.

"They haven't called me from
lost property yet, but I want to
go to the station to look for my
luggage..."

"Very well. Madame de
Pompadour and I are coming
with you. If the luggage is not
there, we are going to give you
a guided tour of Paris."

Knowing that Michel is coming
with me gives me peace of
mind. I even find that Madame
de Pompadour is friendlier
now.

Nous allons à la gare, mais l'homme du bureau des objets trouvés n'a pas mes bagages.

We go to the station, but the man in the lost and found office doesn't have my luggage.

5 Je suis très déçue. Dans le bureau des objets trouvés, on trouve beaucoup de choses différentes : des valises de tailles et de formes diverses,
10 des parapluies de toutes les couleurs, des chaussures perdues, des vestes et des gants dépareillés.

I am very disappointed. In the lost and found office there are lots of different things: suitcases of various sizes and shapes, umbrellas of all colors, lost shoes, jackets and mismatched gloves.

15 Je vois aussi un vélo avec un panier, un jeu d'échecs, une guitare sans cordes et des livres dans de nombreuses langues différentes.
20

I also see a bicycle with a basket, a chess set, a guitar without strings, and books in many different languages.

— Je t'appelle si je trouve ton bagage, dit l'homme du bureau.

"I'll call you if I find your luggage," says the man in the office.

25 Il regarde Michel qui m'attend dehors et me demande :
— Tu as bien dormi ? Je lui dit oui.

He looks at Michel who is waiting for me outside and asks me, "Did you sleep well?" I say yes.

30 — Très bien, répond l'homme du bureau des objets trouvés.
— Michel est une bonne personne.

"Very well," replies the man from the lost and found office. "Michel is a good person.

C'était un banquier important,
un homme avec beaucoup
d'influence, mais...

5   L'homme ne termine pas sa
phrase car Michel s'approche.

— Ce n'est pas là ? demande
Michel. Eh bien, dans ce cas,
Paris nous attend.
10

Je remercie l'homme du bureau
des objets perdus et je sors avec
Michel.

15   — Michel, je suis très
reconnaissante de ta générosité,
mais que pouvons-nous faire
dans cette ville sans argent ?

20   Michel soupire.
— Tu n'as rien appris hier
soir ? Il rit et dit :
— Viens, je vais te montrer
« Paris Gratuit ». Aujourd'hui,
25   c'est samedi, alors nous allons
d'abord au marché.

Nous traversons Paris à pied.
Michel dit que le marché n'est
30   pas loin, mais qu'il doit
marcher lentement parce qu'il a
mal à la jambe.

Before, he used to be an
important banker, a man with a
lot of influence, but...”

The man does not finish his
sentence because Michel is
approaching.
“It’s not there?” Michel asks.
“Well, ok then, in that case
Paris awaits us.”

I thank the man in the lost
property office and go out with
Michel.

“Michel, I am very grateful for
your generosity, but what can
we do in this city without
money?”

Michel sighs.
“Didn't you learn anything last
night?” He laughs and says,
“Come, I'm going to show you
Free Paris. Today is Saturday
so first let’s go to the market.”

We cross Paris on foot. Michel
says the market is not far, but
he has to walk slowly because
his leg hurts.

— Je vieillis, Joanna. Tout mon corps me fait mal : mon cou, mes bras, mes jambes, mes genoux, mon dos... Chaque os de mon corps me fait mal. Je suis une vraie épave.

— Et tu n'as pas de famille pour s'occuper de toi ? je demande. Mais je réalise immédiatement mon erreur et me sens gênée.

Si Michel avait une famille, il ne vivrait pas seul dans la rue.

Michel me regarde et hésite avant de dire :
— J'ai un fils mais il ne me parle pas. Et... Il regarde le sol pensivement. Et... J'ai un petit-fils. Il s'appelle Luc, mais il vit loin, dans le nord de Paris. Bien que parfois…

— Oui... ? je dis avec curiosité.

— Parfois, je vais au parc avec lui. Mais c'est trop loin pour marcher.

"I'm getting old, Joanna. My whole body hurts: my neck, my arms, my legs, my knees, my back... Each and every one of my bones hurts. I'm a real wreck."

"And you don't have any family to take care of you?" I ask him. But I quickly realise my mistake and feel embarrassed.

If Michel had a family, he wouldn't live alone on the streets.

Michel looks at me and hesitates before saying: "I have a son but he doesn't talk to me. And…" He looks at the floor thoughtfully, "and… I have a grandson. His name is Luc, but he lives far away, in the north of Paris. Although sometimes..."

"Yes ... ?" I say, curious.

"Sometimes, I go to the park with him. But it is too far to walk.

Je n'ai presque jamais assez d'argent pour prendre le bus, le métro ou un taxi.

I hardly ever have enough money to take the bus, the underground, or a taxi."

5   C'est très triste, dis-je.

"That's very sad," I say.

Je pense à ma mère et à mon père. Ils ne savent pas où je suis et ils doivent être très
10 tristes, comme Michel.

I think of my mum and dad. They don't know where I am and they must be very sad, like Michel.

— Ça me fait mal au cœur, dis-je sans le vouloir.

"My heart hurts," I say unintentionally.

15 — Moi aussi, dit Michel, puis il prend une grande inspiration et dit :
— Nous sommes arrivés au marché, Joanna.
20

"Me too," Michel says and then takes a deep breath and says,

"We've reached the market, Joanna."

Le marché s'appelle Le Marché Bastille. Les gens y vendent toutes sortes de choses : de la nourriture, des vêtements, des
25 bijoux, des œuvres d'art, des antiquités…

The market is called *Le Marché Bastille.* Here people sell all kinds of things: there are food, clothes, jewelry, works of art, antiques...

C'est incroyable.

It's incredible.

30 — Tu as faim, Joanna ? demande-t-il.

"Are you hungry, Joanna?" He asks me.

— Toujours, je réponds en
riant.

— J'ai des amis ici. Quand
j'étais banquier, je venais ici
faire des courses très souvent.
Cependant, maintenant, je viens
ici pour vendre des objets que
je trouve dans la rue de temps
en temps.

Nous entrons dans une zone de
marché où il y a beaucoup de
nourriture. Plusieurs personnes
saluent Michel.

Ici, tous les étals proposent des
aliments locaux à déguster.

Les touristes savourent les
spécialités de chaque étal. Il y a
du fromage, des gâteaux, de la
viande grillée, des fruits et des
pains au chocolat !

Une femme travaillant à l'étal
m'offre un morceau de pain au
chocolat et il est vraiment
délicieux.

Nous essayons de nombreux
plats typiques en nous
promenant sur le marché.

"Always," I answer, laughing.

"I have friends here. When I
was a banker, I used to come
shopping very often. However,
now I come to sell things that I
find on the street from time to
time."

We enter an area of the market
where there is a lot of food.
Several people greet Michel.

Here all the stalls have local
food to taste.

Tourists are savouring the
specialties of each stall. There's
cheese, cake, roast meat, fruit,
and *pains au chocolat!*

A woman who works at the
stall offers me a piece of *pain
au chocolat* and it is truly
delicious.

We try many typical dishes
while we walk around the
market.

Après le marché, Michel
m'emmène à l'église Saint-
Étienne-du-Mont.

5 Il fait frais à l'intérieur et nous
décidons de nous asseoir sur
l'un des bancs près de l'autel et
de nous reposer un moment.

10 — Es-tu religieuse, Joanna ?
me susurre Michel.

Je dis non.
— Et toi ? je lui demande.
15

— Oui et non. Parfois je parle à
Dieu...

— Et qu'est-ce que tu lui dis ?
20

— Je lui dis que j'aimerais voir
Luc plus souvent. J'ai perdu
tout ce que j'avais en un jour -
tout, même mes chaussettes - et
25 maintenant j'ai peur de perdre
aussi mon petit-fils. Ça ne me
dérange pas de vivre dans la
rue, mais ne pas voir le petit
Luc, mon petit-fils, me fait de
30 la peine, vraiment de la peine.

After the market, Michel takes
me to *Saint-Etienne-du-Mont*
church.

It's cool inside and we decide to
sit on one of the benches near
the altar and rest for a while.

"Are you religious, Joanna?"
Michel whispers to me.

I say no.
"And you?" I ask him.

"Yes and no. Sometimes I talk
to God ..."

"And what do you say to him?"

"I tell him I'd like to see Luc
more often. I lost everything I
had in one day - everything,
even my socks - and now I'm
afraid of losing my grandson
too. I don't mind living on the
streets, but not seeing little Luc,
my grandson, hurts me, it hurts
me a lot."

Après la visite de l'église, nous nous promenons dans le Jardin des Plantes.

5 — Tu as aimé « Paris Gratuit » ? il me demande avec un grand sourire.

— C'est vraiment
10 impressionnant. Je me suis éclatée. Mais maintenant j'ai mal aux pieds à force de marcher !

After visiting the church, we walk through the *Jardin des Plantes.*

"Did you like "*Free Paris*"? he asks me with a beaming smile.

"It is really impressive. I've had a blast. But the truth is that now my feet hurt from so much walking!"

CHAPTER 6

Les objets perdus.

Il est quatre heures et demie de l'après-midi lorsque nous décidons de retourner en direction de Rue de Rivoli.

It is half past four in the afternoon when we decide to return to *Rue de Rivoli.*

5

Je n'ai ni bagage ni argent, mais j'ai de nouveaux amis et j'ai passé une nuit et une journée très intéressantes à Paris.

I have neither luggage nor money, but I have new friends and I've spent a very interesting night and day in Paris.

10

Michel a raison : il y a beaucoup de choses que l'on peut faire à Paris sans argent.

Michel is right: there are lots of things that can be done in Paris without money.

15 Nous passons devant le musée du Louvre et je regarde ses portes en pensant aux personnes élégantes que j'ai vues la veille.

We pass in front of the *Louvre* Museum and I look towards its doors thinking of the elegant people I saw the night before.

20

Oui, il y a beaucoup de choses que l'on peut faire gratuitement à Paris, mais pas toutes…

Yes, it is true that you can do lots of things for free in Paris, but not everything...

25 Michel me regarde et me dit :
—Tu t'intéresses à l'art, petite ?

Michel looks at me and says:
"Are you interested in art, child?"
I say yes.

Je dis oui.

30 — Le Musée du Louvre est très célèbre. J'aimerais vraiment le visiter un jour. Je reviendrai quand j'aurai de l'argent.

"The *Louvre* Museum is very famous. I would very much like to visit it one day. I will come back when I have money."

Michel rit.
— Viens avec moi, Joanna. Je
veux te montrer quelque chose.
Nous allons vers le musée,
5 mais je ne comprends pas ce
que Michel va faire.

Le musée a l'air très élégant et
très cher. Autour du musée, il y
10 a un parc avec des affiches
promouvant diverses
expositions d'art.

Nous arrivons à l'entrée du
15 musée et des agents de sécurité
nous regardent.

Je me sens honteuse. Moi, une
fille sans le sou qui ne s'est pas
20 douchée depuis trois jours, et
mon ami, un sans-abri avec un
chat sur ses épaules.

On dirait qu'ils vont nous
25 arrêter, mais lorsque nous
arrivons à la porte, un des
agents salue Michel.

— M. Michel Berthier. Ça fait
30 longtemps ! Quelle joie de vous
voir ! Comment allez-vous,
monsieur ?

Michel laughs.
"Come with me, Joanna. I want
to show you something."
We are heading towards the
museum, but I don't understand
what Michel is going to do.

The museum looks very elegant
and very expensive. Around the
museum there is a park where
there are promotional posters
for various art exhibitions.

We arrive at the entrance of the
museum and there are security
guards looking at us.

I feel embarrassed. Me, a
penniless girl who hasn't
showered in three days, and my
friend, a homeless man with a
cat on his shoulders.

It looks like they are going to
stop us, but when we get to the
door, one of the guards greets
Michel.

"Mr Michel Berthier. Long
time no see! What a joy to see
you! How are you, sir?"

— Eh bien, merci Laurent.
Mon amie Joanna veut voir le
musée, d'accord ?

5 — Bien sûr, monsieur. Vous
êtes toujours le bienvenu,
répond l'agent en ouvrant la
porte.

10 Nous entrons dans le musée et
je vois qu'il est immense.
L'entrée est moderne, mais il y
a des œuvres d'art de toutes les
époques.
15

D'un côté de l'entrée, il y a un
restaurant et une boutique, et de
l'autre, je vois des salles et des
couloirs qui partent dans toutes
20 les directions.

— Tu connais les agents de
sécurité ? je demande à Michel.

25 — Eh bien, oui... Avant, quand
j'étais banquier, je travaillais
beaucoup avec les directeurs du
musée. Ils me connaissent bien.

30 Je suis impressionnée.

"Well, thanks Laurent. My
friend Joanna wants to see the
museum, okay?"

"Of course, sir. You are always
welcome," answers the guard,
opening the door.

We enter the museum and I see
that it is huge. The entrance is
modern, but there are works of
art from all eras.

On one side of the entrance
there is a restaurant and a shop,
and on the other I see rooms
and corridors that go off in all
directions.

"Do you know the guards?" I
ask Michel.

"Well, yes… Before, when I
was a banker, I worked a lot
with the directors of the
museum. They know me well."

I'm impressed.

— Quelles affaires Michel
avait-il avec les directeurs du
Musée du Louvre ?
Et comment se fait-il qu'il
dorme maintenant dans la rue, à
l'ombre des magnifiques
bâtiments du musée ?

— C'est pour ça qu'ils nous
laissent entrer gratuitement ?
je demande.

Michel sourit.
— Non, ma fille. Le premier
samedi du mois, le musée du
Louvre est gratuit pour tous.

L'art est pour tout le monde,
pas seulement pour les riches.

Michel m'emmène dans
plusieurs salles où je vois des
œuvres d'art de Léonard de
Vinci, de Delacroix, de Titien,
de Véronèse, de Géricault et
bien d'autres.

Je me trouve devant l'entrée de
l'une des salles et je vois qu'il y
a une plaque dorée qui dit :
« Salle M. Berthier ».

*What business did Michel have
with the directors of the Louvre
Museum?
And how can it be that he now
sleeps on the street in the
shadow of the magnificent
museum buildings?*

"Is that why they let us in for
free?" I ask him.

Michel smiles.
"No, child. On the first
Saturday of the month, the
Louvre Museum is free for
everyone."

Art is for everyone, not just the
rich.

Michel takes me to various
rooms where I see works of art
Léonard da Vinci, Delacroix,
Titien, Véronèse, Géricault and
many more.

I stop in front of the entrance of
one of the rooms and see that
there is a gold plate that says
"The M. Berthier Hall."

Nous entrons et voyons une œuvre d'art très ancienne représentant une jeune fille qui coud.

5

— C'est mon œuvre d'art préférée. Elle s'appelle *La Dentellière,* dit Michel.
— Cela me rappelle beaucoup
10 mon enfance quand je regardais ma mère et ma soeur coudre. Il y a beaucoup de calme et de sérénité ici, comme chez moi quand j'étais enfant.
15

Soudain, mon téléphone vibre. J'ai un message. C'est l'homme du bureau des objets perdus.

20 — Il a mes bagages !

— Je dois aller à la gare ! dis-je à Michel avec enthousiasme.
— Ils ont mes bagages ! Enfin,
25 mon passeport, mon argent, mes affaires ! Merci pour tout, Michel, mais je dois y aller...

30 — Très bien, ma fille, je viens avec toi ? demande-t-il.

We enter and see a very old work of art of a young lady sewing.

"It's my favorite work of art. It's called *The Lacemaker*" says Michel.
"It reminds me a lot of my childhood when I used to watch my mother and sister sewing. There is a lot of calm and serenity here, just like in my home when I was a child.

Suddenly my phone vibrates. I have a message. It's the man from the lost and found office.

He has my luggage!

"I have to go to the station!", I tell Michel excitedly.
"They have my luggage! Finally, my passport, my money, my things! Thanks for everything Michel, but I have to go..."

"How nice, child! Shall I come with you?" He asks me.

Je le regarde et je secoue la
tête.

Il a l'air très fatigué et j'imagine
5   que ses jambes, ses genoux, ses
chevilles lui font mal.

Le pauvre !

10   Mais je suis tellement contente
que je cours jusqu'à la gare.

J'ai passé un bon moment avec
Michel, mais maintenant j'ai
15   envie de prendre une douche,
de manger dans un restaurant et
de sortir avec ma meilleure
amie à Toulouse.

20   — Peut-être que je peux
prendre le train ce soir ?

Lorsque j'arrive à la gare, il est
déjà dix-neuf heures quinze et
25   l'homme du bureau des objets
trouvés m'attend.

Il a mes bagages. Je le
30   remercie. Je suis un peu
nerveuse.

I look at him and shake my
head.

He seems very tired and I
imagine his legs, knees, ankles
must hurt.

Poor man.

But I feel so excited that I run
to the station.

I've had a great time with
Michel, but now I want to
shower, eat in a restaurant and
go out with my best friend in
Toulouse.

*Maybe I can catch the train
tonight?*

By the time I get to the station,
it's already quarter past seven in
the evening and the man from
the lost property office is
waiting for me.

He has my luggage. I thank
him. I'm a little nervous.

— Toutes mes affaires seront-elles dans les bagages ?

5 Je l'ouvre lentement et, heureusement, mon portefeuille et mon passeport sont à l'intérieur.
Je soupire de soulagement.

10 Maintenant, j'ai de l'argent et des vêtements, et ma bouteille d'eau aussi.

L'homme sourit.
15 — As-tu tout ce dont tu as besoin ? il me demande.

Je regarde les objets perdus dans son bureau.
20
— Non... Je n'ai pas tout. J'ai besoin de quelque chose d'autre... Et je me demande si tu peux m'aider, lui dis-je.

Will all my things still be in the luggage?

I open it slowly and luckily my wallet and passport are inside.

I sigh in relief.

Now I have money and clothes, and my water bottle too.

The man smiles. "Do you have everything you need?" He asks me.

I look at the lost items in his office.

"No ... I don't have everything. I need something else... and I wonder if you can help me," I say.

CHAPTER 7

Quand je rentre au camp, il est déjà vingt heures.

Michel et Madame de Pompadour sont au centre du camp et discutent avec leurs amis.

Je laisse quelques affaires derrière les tentes et je m'approche du groupe.

Michel me voit et me dit :
— Tu es de retour ! Il est surpris.

Même Madame de Pompadour a l'air surprise.
— Tu veux du thé ? demande-t-il. Je dis oui et je m'assois avec eux.

— Je vois que tu as déjà tes bagages, dit l'ami de Michel en pointant son doigt.

—Oui, oui. Et tout est là. J'ai mes vêtements, mon passeport, mon argent et… même ma bouteille d'eau !

When I return to the camp, it is already eight in the evening.

Michel and Madame de Pompadour are in the centre of the camp chatting with their friends.

I leave some things behind the tents and go over to the group.

Michel sees me and says:
"You're back!" He is surprised.

Even Madame de Pompadour seems surprised.
"Do you want tea?" He asks me. I say yes and sit down with them.

"I see you already have your luggage," says a friend of Michel, pointing a finger.

"Yes, yes. And everything is inside. Now I have my clothes, passport, money and… even my water bottle!"

J'ai aussi appelé mes parents.
Maintenant ils savent où je
suis... et que je suis saine et
sauve. J'ai eu tort de partir sans
5 rien dire.

— Tu ne choisis pas ta famille,
ma fille. C'est un cadeau de
Dieu pour toi, dit Michel en me
10 passant une tasse de thé.

Le chat se frotte à mes jambes
avec son corps.

15 —Et quand vas-tu à Toulouse ?

— Demain. Je vais prendre le
train à huit heures.
20
— J'en suis ravi, dit Michel
avec un sourire chaleureux.
Madame de Pompadour me
regarde avec de grands yeux. Je
25 la caresse et elle commence à
ronronner.

— Je veux vous inviter à dîner,
dis-je à Michel et à ses amis. Et
30 j'ai une surprise pour toi
Michel. Tu viens ?

I have also called my parents.
Now they know where I am...
and that I am safe and sound. I
was wrong to leave without
saying anything."

"You don't choose your family,
child. They are a gift from God
to you," Michel tells me,
handing me a cup of tea.

The cat is rubbing my legs with
her body.

"And when are you going to
Toulouse ?"

"Tomorrow. I'm going to catch
the train at eight in the
morning."
"I'm glad," Michel says with a
warm smile. Madame de
Pompadour looks at me with
big eyes. I stroke her and she
begins to purr.

"I want to invite you to dinner,"
I tell Michel and his friends.
"And I have a surprise for you
Michel. You coming?"

— Une surprise ? Bien, alors d'accord, bien sûr que je viens.

"A surprise? Well, okay, of course I'm coming."

Michel ramasse son chat et me suit derrière les tentes.

Michel takes the cat and follows me behind the tents.

On voit qu'il est fatigué parce que son boitement est encore pire qu'avant.

I can see that he is tired because his limp seems even worse than before.

— Eh bien, qu'y a-t-il, mon enfant ?

"Well, what is it, child?"

Je lui montre le vélo.
— C'est pour toi, Michel. Maintenant, tu peux voir ton petit-fils quand tu veux. Il y a même un panier pour Madame de Pompadour.

I show him the bicycle.
"It's for you, Michel. Now you can see your grandson whenever you want." It even has a basket for Madame de Pompadour.

Michel hésite un instant.
— Ma fille... Je ne peux pas l'accepter. Tu n'as pas beaucoup d'argent et… et…

Michel hesitates for a moment.
"Child... I can't accept it. You don't have much money and... and..."

— L'homme du bureau des objets trouvés me l'a donné. Le vélo était dans son bureau depuis deux ans.

"The man from the lost and found office gave it to me." The bike had been in his office for two years.

Elle avait juste besoin d'un peu d'huile et maintenant elle est comme neuve.

It just needed a little oil and now it's as good as new.

— C'est juste que... Je ne sais pas quoi dire, ma fille...

"I just... I don't know what to say, child..."

— C'est comme tu dis : les meilleures choses de la vie sont gratuites.

"It's like you say it: the best things in life are free."

La famille, l'indépendance, la liberté. Ces choses n'ont pas de prix.

Family, independence, freedom. Those things are priceless.

— Tu as raison, mon enfant, tu as raison. Michel met Madame de Pompadour dans le panier et monte sur le vélo.

"You are right, child, you are right." Michel puts Madame de Pompadour in the basket and gets on the bicycle.

Le chat regarde Michel et s'assied confortablement.

The cat looks at Michel and sits down comfortably.

— Hé Madame de Pompadour, que penses-tu d'une promenade dans le nord de Paris demain matin ?

"Hey Madame de Pompadour, how about we go for a ride to the north of Paris tomorrow morning?"

— C'est génial, Michel ! dis-je.
— Mais tu viens avec moi maintenant ?

"That's great, Michel!" I say. "But are you coming with me now?"

— Où ça ? demande-t-il.

"Where to?" he asks me.

—Allons faire des courses. Je veux trouver la nourriture la plus *moche* de Paris.

"We're going shopping. I want to find the *ugliest* food in Paris."

www.ingramcontent.com/pod-product-compliance
Lightning Source LLC
LaVergne TN
LVHW051056180726
843512LV00019B/1495